Your Education Research Project Handbook

Visit the *Your Education Research Project Handbook*
Companion Website at **www.pearsoned.co.uk/colesmcgrath**
to find valuable **student** learning material including:

- Examples of interviews, questionnaires and observation schedules
- Examples of letters to research participants
- A sample assignment
- A planning checklist
- Examples of how to analyse quantitative and qualitative data
- Statistics and research examples – exercises and answers

PEARSON

We work with leading authors to develop the strongest
educational materials in education and study skills, bringing
cutting-edge thinking and best learning practice to a
global market.

Under a range of well-known imprints, including Longman
we craft high quality print and electronic publications
which help readers to understand and apply their content,
whether studying or at work.

To find out more about the complete range of our
publishing, please visit us on the World Wide Web at:
www.pearsoned.co.uk

Your Education Research Project Handbook

Anthony Coles
Birmingham City University

Jim McGrath
Birmingham City University

Longman
is an imprint of

Harlow, England • London • New York • Boston • San Francisco • Toronto • Sydney • Singapore • Hong Kong
Tokyo • Seoul • Taipei • New Delhi • Cape Town • Madrid • Mexico City • Amsterdam • Munich • Paris • Milan

Pearson Education Limited
Edinburgh Gate
Harlow
Essex
CM20 2JE
England

and Associated Companies throughout the world

Visit us on the World Wide Web at:
www.pearsoned.co.uk

First published 2010

© Pearson Education Limited 2010

ISBN: 978–1–4082–2124–2

British Library Cataloguing-in-Publication Data
A catalogue record for this book is available from the British Library.

Library of Congress Cataloging-in-Publication Data
A catalog record for this book is available from the Library of Congress.

10 9 8 7 6 5 4 3 2 1
13 12 11 10 09

Typeset in 10/15pt Arial Light by 30
Printed in Great Britain by Henry Ling Ltd., at the Dorset Press, Dorchester, Dorset

The publisher's policy is to use paper manufactured from sustainable forests.

Contents

About the authors   vii
Introduction   viii
Acknowledgements   xiv

Tutorial 1 Getting started   1

Tutorial 2 How to structure your research report   17

Tutorial 3 Writing your literature review   37

Tutorial 4 Choosing your research methodology   55

Tutorial 5 Research strategies – case studies, action research
                and surveys   77

Tutorial 6 Gathering your data – interviews and observations   97

Tutorial 7 Gathering your data – documents and questionnaires   117

Tutorial 8 Analysis of qualitative data   131

Tutorial 9 Analysis of quantitative data   149

Tutorial 10 Some final advice   173

Glossary of terms   189
Bibliography   193
Index   195

About the authors

Anthony Coles is Reader in Post-compulsory Education and MA Education Course Director at Birmingham City University. Much of his teaching involves research skills and supporting teachers in their professional development. Anthony is particularly interested in supporting students to overcome any fears they may have about the use of quantitative methods in education research.

Jim McGrath currently teaches research skills and education management and leadership on a number of undergraduate and postgraduate courses. As someone who gained all his qualifications by part-time study, Jim is almost as passionate about working with part-time students as he is in supporting his beloved West Bromwich Albion.

Introduction

Whom is this book for?

There are many good books available that deal with educational research. So why do we need another one? We believe that there is a need for a new kind of research textbook. One that minimises the use of jargon, provides user-friendly guidance on how to design and carry out a small scale piece of research and recognises that many first time researchers find the process of research stressful.

Between us we have nearly 40 years' experience of supervising undergraduate and postgraduate students' research projects, dissertations and theses. We are aware that many students find undertaking their first piece of research a frightening experience. After all isn't research only carried out by academics and scientists? Nothing could be further from the truth. We all do research every day, but we don't call it that. For example when you buy a new car don't you read up on the various models available, visit a few car showrooms and speak to someone who already owns the model of car that you are thinking of buying? That is research. You are discovering information about an issue that is of importance to you.

So what is it about research that frightens people? We think that there are two main problems. Firstly, students think that research has to be 'original' and that they have to 'discover new knowledge'. The truth is much more mundane. At undergraduate and Master's level you can research a topic that people have been looking at for years – e.g. classroom management, the motivation of students or mentoring of trainee teachers – and still achieve a very good pass. So if a topic has already been researched to death what is the point of researching it again? It is valuable because what you discover will be new knowledge to you and it will inform your thinking and professional practice (we hope!). You will also have learnt a valuable new skill. Secondly, the language of research, the jargon used, frightens people – e.g. research methodology, triangulation, reliability, sampling sets and validity. No wonder people find it difficult to relate research to what they do in the classroom or office.

The sole aim of this book is to simplify the research process. We aim to tell you everything you need to know to carry out successfully a small scale piece of empirical research. That is research, which involves collecting data from sources other than just books. *The book is not designed to meet the needs of students undertaking 'conceptually based research' where the researcher is solely concerned with exploring ideas and theories although parts of it might be useful to such researchers.*

We explain the major stages in the research process from initial idea to finished assignment in a clear and unambiguous manner. We simplify the issues so that you can get a firm grip on the key ideas but the work is not simplistic. Einstein said that great art was the expression of complex ideas in the simplest possible form. It is this kind of user-friendly simplicity that we seek. In addition we address the type of concerns and fears that new researchers may have at each stage of the process.

Format and style of book

The book is written from the viewpoint of Sam, a mature student who is working on a part-time programme. This means that the process of research is examined through the eyes of the student and not those of an academic dispensing words of wisdom. We believe that this approach helps us to simplify and make transparent the research process. The gender and age of Sam is never specified. This was a conscious decision. Sam is an amalgam of the hundreds of students that we have had the pleasure to work with over the years and we would invite you to create your own back story for the character.

Each chapter is based on a single tutorial meeting and deals with one aspect of the research process. The topics covered are those that you would find in any research programme. To avoid a purely theoretical discussion examples of how to choose and apply research methodologies and tools are provided in the context of Sam's own research interests. It is essential that as you read you constantly consider 'how is this relevant to my research and how would I apply it in practice'? Within each chapter, you will find:

- extracts from Sam's reflective journal;
- a review of the tutorial meeting between Sam and Dr. Richard Reed, research supervisor;
- a summary of key learning points arising from the tutorial and agreed action points;
- a diagrammatical overview of the tutorial summarising the issues discussed and showing their interrelationships;

- handouts provided by Dr. Reed during the tutorial;
- advice on additional reading.

In addition to the above, a list of contents is provided at the start of each tutorial together with a short statement outlining the aims of the tutorial. However, the order of the contents is indicative only. This is because the nature of a tutorial means that the discussion may return to the same topic more than once and Sam's reflections are inevitably retrospective.

A glossary of key terms is provided at the end of the book which you may wish to refer to for clarification. Each key term has been **highlighted** in the text when first used.

As the size of this book is limited additional materials can be found at **www. pearsoned.co.uk/colesmcgrath**; these include examples of data collection tools, a series of checklists that can be used at each stage of the research process and a copy of a completed research project on 'Children's perception of their own safety' by Tracey Grainger. Best of all the entire site is free. We would urge you to log on.

Tutorial 1 provides an overview of the research process and suggests how to tackle the problem of drafting usable research questions. Tutorial 2 explains how to structure a research report or dissertation. Tutorial 3 considers the notion of a conceptual framework. Specifically it looks at how to find and evaluate relevant literature and write up that all-important literature review.

Tutorial 4 discusses two popular research methodologies, namely quantitative and qualitative. Both methodologies are defined and their strengths and weaknesses discussed. Additionally, aspects of methodology such as ethics, triangulation, validity and reliability are covered. Tutorial 5 reviews three popular research strategies namely case study, action research and survey. Each is defined and evaluated and guidance given on how to select the most appropriate strategy.

Tutorials 6 and 7 look at four popular data collection tools, namely questionnaires, interviews, observations and documentation. An example of each is provided and guidance given on how to select the most appropriate method for your research.

Tutorial 8 examines how to analyse, evaluate and report qualitative data. A step by step approach guides you through the process of comparing and contrasting data, including making links with the literature review. Tutorial 9 considers how to analyse, evaluate and report quantitative data.

Tutorial 10 provides guidance on how to write up your research and improve your final mark. It also considers such thorny issues as how much is enough analysis and how do you decide which data to relegate to an appendix?

How to use this book

Most people undertaking a research project or dissertation attend a series of taught sessions where they learn about the 'nuts and bolts' of the research process. On completion, they are allocated a supervisor who acts as their guide through the research process. For the purpose of this book, we have combined the roles of teacher and supervisor. Therefore, when Sam turns up for a tutorial Dr. Reed provides a mixture of taught input and supervision. We realise that this is unusual but it enables us to discuss the full range of research issues faced by new researchers from the student's perspective. We would encourage you to think of this book as an addition to your research notes. So don't be afraid to annotate it and make it your own.

So how might you use the book? Assuming that your course has a taught research programme you may wish to:

- Read the relevant chapter or chapters before attending a taught session on the same issues. This will familiarise you with the key concepts and enable you to clarify anything that you are unsure of with your lecturer.

- Read the appropriate chapter after a session. This will reinforce the learning that has already taken place and provide a different perspective on the issues.

- Use the summary of each tutorial's main points as the basis for your own notes and/or for quick revision.

- Study the overview diagram in each tutorial to identify and understand the interconnectedness of the research process. Visual learners may wish to study the diagram before reading the relevant tutorial in order to obtain an overview of the issues discussed.

- Use Sam's action points to guide you in what you need to do at each stage of the research process.

- Use the book as your primary learning resource when you have missed a session entirely, or found a lesson particularly difficult.

- Follow up the further reading recommendations provided at the end of each chapter.

If you don't have access to taught research sessions than you can use this book as your primary teaching aid and supplement it using the further reading recommendations given at the end of each chapter. We are conscious that long reading lists can demotivate rather than inspire students and for that reason we have restricted our recommendations to the following three texts.

Cohen, L., Mannion, L. and Morrison, K. (2007) *Research Methods in Education (6th Edition)*. Routledge Falmer: London.

Denscombe, M. (2008) *The Good Research Guide (3rd Edition)*. OUP: Buckingham.

Newby, P. (2010) *Research Methods for Education*. Longman, Pearson: Harlow.

When following up a reference you should decide how much of the recommended chapter you need to read (some, most, all) and develop the habit of using the book's index to find key terms and ideas.

Occasionally, in the text, you will find a reference dated 20xx. This is a fictitious reference used solely by Dr Reed for illustrative purposes.

As the book deals with the practical and emotional problems encountered by novice researchers, you can also use it as a source of comfort and impartial advice. On a wet dark evening when you are convinced that what you have written is utter rubbish it is comforting to know that every researcher goes through this stage, even those of us who have been doing it for a very long time.

Health warning

This book promotes a widely used approach to conducting and reporting empirical research, however it is essential that you familiarise yourself with the requirements of your own institution, particularly in relation to the specific assessment criteria and ethical requirements relating to your assignment. This is essential as there are variations in custom and practice across different institutions, which if not observed could result in a reduced mark for your work.

We wish you the very best of luck with your research and if you have any suggestions for how we could make this book more useful to the novice researcher please contact us.

Jim McGrath

Anthony Coles

Birmingham City University, 2009

Dedication

For Eija, Helen and Michael and in memory of my brother Tony McGrath.

For Jane, Bea and William for tolerating the back of my laptop for the last six months.

Acknowledgements

It was Tracey Granger's well written and interesting BA (Hons.) Education Studies Dissertation that prompted us to select child safety as the focus for the research project discussed in this book. We would like to thank Tracey for her permission to use her dissertation as the basis for some of the content on the website that accompanies this book.

We would like to thank our editor Catherine Yates at Pearson Education for her support and encouragement at every stage of the writing process. Not everyone is willing to champion a new and unusual approach to writing for students. We were lucky to find you.

And finally many thanks to Katy Robinson at Pearson Education, who kept us all on track.

GETTING STARTED

Aim of tutorial

To provide you with an overview of the research process and guidance on how to define the focus of your research and draft suitable research questions.

Contents

→ Finding a focus for your research

→ Designing your research questions

→ Disseminating your findings

→ Gaining acccess and the value of insider research

→ Planning your research

Note: Key terms have been **highlighted** in the text when first used. A definition of these terms is provided in the glossary at the end of the book.

Sam's reflection

13 September, lunchtime

Mrs. Storm the Course Director reminded us all last week that we need to keep a reflective journal as part of our coursework for a minimum of three months. Needless to say I'd forgotten all about it. Why do lecturers have to invent additional time-wasting jobs? Don't they know that I have a full-time job and a social life? Still, I want to pass the course so I'll have to do it. Luckily I start my tutorials on the 15th with Dr. Reed, so I can base my journal around my learning on the Research Project Module. That should give me enough information to reflect upon.

I have to say that I find the whole idea of undertaking research strange. I mean I know that I'm not stupid, but I'd never describe myself as an academic. Being a researcher is not part of who I am. I never saw myself doing research at university. It sounds so formal. If I'm honest, I'm both excited and scared. I mean if the lecturer asks a question in the classroom you can keep your head down and avoid answering, but on a one-to-one basis with your supervisor there'll be no hiding place. He'll quickly see how little I know and I will end up making a fool of myself.

Oh, why did I choose the research option? Still it's too late to back out now.

I wonder what Dr. Reed will be like? Hope he's not one of those academics that try to overcomplicate things.

Barry Allan was telling me that when he did this course he found it really difficult to take notes and listen to what his supervisor was saying at the same time. He ended up recording each session. I think I'll do that. It means I can concentrate on what's said and not worry about missing anything, 'cos I can always listen to the tape. I'd better give the good Doctor a ring and see if he is happy with me taping his tutorials.

* * *

Dr. Reed sounded friendly enough when I phoned him. He asked if I was free to pop round and see him tonight for an informal chat. He's in the Baxter Building. That's miles from the Kent Car Park. I hope it stops raining before six.

13 September, evening

Well that wasn't as bad as I thought it would be. Dr. Reed, 'call me Richard', seemed really friendly. He wanted to know all about me. What I did at work. What modules I had previously studied. What my professional interests are. What I liked to do in my spare time. He said that this background information helped him understand each student as a person. Of course he could just be nosey.

Funnily enough while he was trying to find out about me I was checking him out. Judging by the poster by his desk he's a football fan. West Bromwich Albion by the look of it. Poor soul. With a team like that he must be constantly depressed. But it's probably best if I avoid insulting them. He also has a mini library in his room. I wonder if he's read every book or if they are there just for show? He's also an untidy so-and-so if his desk is anything to go by. And he could do with a hair cut.

Richard was happy for me to record the tutorial. In fact, I think he was quite impressed with the idea. Apparently, some students turn up without even a pen to take notes. How can they hope to remember what a tutor says over the course of 45 minutes without some notes? So first things first. Richard asked me to jot down my research questions before I see him on the 15th. That shouldn't take long.

Review of tutorial

Richard was reading his emails when I entered. He looked up and smiled. 'So our meeting didn't put you off then?'

'No, but tonight might,' I said with more feeling than I had intended.

'Grab a seat' he said and waited for me to get organised. 'When I spoke to you I asked you to identify a topic or issue that you wanted to find out more about and jot-down some research questions. What have you come up with?'

'Well, I thought that I would look at children's perception of safety when attending school.'

'That's a good topic. What age group are you looking at?'

'Seven to 11.'

'OK. So why are you interested in their perceptions of safety?'

'The school I work in has been doing some work in this area with parents and I'd like to identify ways that we can make the process of attending school less frightening for children,' I said more confidently than I felt.

'Fine. I always like it when someone can do a piece of research that they are interested in and which their employers support. It means that you can legitimately do some of your research during working hours and you are likely to get support from your line manager and colleagues. Have you thought about the focus for your research?'

'I'm sorry?' I said, unsure what he meant.

'What I mean is which aspect or aspects of safety do you wish to concentrate on. For example are you interested in the children travelling to and from school or only in school?'

'Both. I want to discover what their perceptions are about safety during the whole school day from when they leave the house to when they return.'

'Good, you've clearly thought about the scope of your research. Effectively you're doing an **empirical** study on the children's perception of their own safety, travelling to and from school, in the classroom, among other children and in the playground. Is that correct?'

'Yes, that is about it.'

'In which case you now need to identify your research questions.'

'You mean like, "How safe do children feel in the classroom?" Or "why do children feel unsafe travelling to and from school?"'

'Not quite. Your questions sound like they have a specific answer.'

'They're supposed to have a specific answer aren't they?' I said defensively, 'They're questions.'

'Ahh! Now there is the problem,' he said smiling. A research question needn't end with a question mark. The use of a question mark implies that there is a single answer and that you intend to find it. For example, your question implies that the children have a single view of safety which can be easily communicated, when in reality each child will have a different profile of concerns depending on their personalities and the situation they find themselves in. You'd be much safer saying "I wish to explore to what degree children feel safe in the classroom and identify their concerns". This is an open-ended question and allows you to explore the various issues that are at play. It also means that you don't have to provide a single "correct" interpretation of the data.'

Sam's reflection

15 September

We then spent 10 minutes discussing how in social science research we can never fully understand why people behave in certain ways or why events occur because there are so many different factors involved in even the simplest social interaction. For example, why did the teacher lose her patience with an unruly child? Was it because of the child's behaviour or because the teacher was unwell? There are too many variables at play, many of which we are unaware of, for us to claim any causal relationship as Richard put it. I must admit I was surprised when he said that. Thinking about it now, this was probably the most important thing that I learnt in the session. Research in the ➡

social sciences, especially the type that I'm undertaking, isn't about finding a specific answer or proving something, it's about understanding what 's going on in a particular situation. Somehow, knowing that I don't have to prove something has given me greater freedom in what I can do. In some way it seems to have made my research more doable.

Review of tutorial

'Research questions are difficult to write and there are a number of things that you need to think about. I always suggest that people should start by writing a **focal paragraph**. That's a short piece, no more than a page long – shorter if possible – which outlines the area that you want to research. It explains what you want to find out and you can use it like a compass to keep you on track as the research progresses. From this focal paragraph you draw out your research questions. Three might be enough for a short piece of work, maybe four or five for a longer one such as a project or dissertation, but no more.'

'But if I'm writing 15,000 words won't I need more questions than if I am writing 5000 words?'

'You'd think so, but the truth is that within any research question there will be a number of issues. The more words you have to play with the deeper you can delve into each of these issues. Even a PhD at 80,000 words will probably only have four or five main research questions but each will be explored in great depth.'

'So what you are saying is that as you progress further in your studies you go deeper into each question and the issues within it rather than increase the number of questions.'

'Precisely.'

'So what makes a good research question?' I asked.

'They have to be clear and explicit to both you and your supervisor. Both of you need to know what it is that you're trying to find out. They also have to be doable.

For example, what's wrong with the following question: "I wish to identify what limits the potential of five high achieving students"?'

I wasn't at all sure that I had an answer but suggested, 'It's a bit vague.'

'It's more than a bit vague,' Richard replied. 'How do you define and measure potential, what is meant by high achieving students and what limitations are we talking about? Are they physical, mental, sociological or all three? It is a really complex question that would be a nightmare to research. No, what you have to do is keep it simple, focused and manageable in the timescale available.'

Sam's reflection

16 September

Clearly writing my research questions is not something that I can just dash-off in a spare ten minutes. I need to think about which aspects of safety I'm most interested in. Then I need to write my focal paragraph and think carefully about the precise research questions that I want to investigate. I also need to keep the number of research questions I set myself to a manageable number. Six is too many for a 7500 project, three would be about right.

Review of tutorial

'So you have an idea about what you want to investigate. The next question is who are you going to collect data from?'

'As I said the school has already canvassed the parents so I thought that I would collect data from the children and teachers.'

'And how do you intend to collect the data?'

'There are about 140 children so I thought that I would use a questionnaire and then interview say six teachers.'

'How long will each interview last?'

I hadn't really thought about that so I suggested, 'Half an hour.'

A slight smile touched his lips and he tugged his ear. 'Each half-hour interview will generate about five pages of single spaced A4. That's at least thirty pages of transcripts or about 12,000 words of text. Not to mention all the data from your questionnaires.'

My mouth didn't drop open but it felt as if it had. That much! Never!

'How long is your assignment?' he asked.

'Seven thousand five hundred words,' I replied.

'I'd suggest focussing on the children, but supporting this with say three short structured interviews with teachers, or maybe a focus group. You'll get other opinions when you present your findings.'

'I hadn't planned on presenting my findings. I was just going to give the head a copy of my report.'

'I'd encourage you to share your findings with colleagues, perhaps at a staff training day. It's really important that teachers disseminate their research to colleagues, that way good practice and increased understanding of the issues can be shared. But it's up to you. Anyway I seem to have been doing a lot of talking. Do you have any questions for me?'

'Do I have to include copies of the completed questionnaires and interview transcripts as an appendix in the final work?'

'Some universities ask for that but we just require a blank copy of your questionnaire.'

'How about carrying out research where I work, is that ok?'

'Yes of course it is. Why do you ask?'

'No reason really, I just thought that I might have to carry out the research outside of my normal workplace for it to be acceptable.'

'No there is no such requirement. What you are doing is called "insider research" and we can look at that when we talk about ethics. But I would argue that one of the major strengths of your project is that you have easy access to the people you want to research. That makes life much easier. I once had a student who wanted to research the leadership style of a friend who worked in the Royal Navy. His friend was happy to be observed in action but it took six months for the researcher to get security clearance and permission to board one of Her Majesty's nuclear submarines. Needless to say his assignment was late! So always check that you have access before embarking on the project. You will need to confirm with your line manager that you have permission to carry out the research and that the parents have given their permission for the school to undertake research with the pupils. Normally this isn't a problem.'

Sam's reflection

16 September

It is obvious that I've seriously underestimated the amount of data that I'd collect from six interviews, not to mention the questionnaires. I need to think about the various ways that I might reduce the size of the research. My options include:

- *Sending the teachers a questionnaire rather than interviewing them.*

- *Restricting the research to just pupils.*

- *Only looking at how children perceive safety within the school and exclude consideration of travelling to/from school.*

I need to think some more about this. What's my primary interest?

I was glad to hear that I can carry out the research in my own workplace. I remember a previous lecturer banging on about the need to always carry out research outside your normal environment. His argument was that it helped you to be objective. Clearly Richard disagrees. Maybe I'll ask him about this when I see him next.

Review of tutorial

'Now we're starting to get to grips with the issues,' he said leaning forward. 'We have an idea about the what, the where and the how. The next thing to think about is the when. When are you going to collect your data?'

'I'll have to do it when things are a bit less manic. I was thinking of just before Easter.'

'Remember the hand-in date for this assignment is the 30 June and you'll need time to write up your findings, therefore I suggest that you collect the data a little sooner, maybe mid-term. But you will need the help of your colleagues to distribute, administer and collect in the questionnaires, so time your data gathering to minimise the disruption that your research might cause them. That way they may let you in again! Once you have a date we can start to draw up a research plan and timetable.'

Sam's Reflection

16 September

We spent the final few minutes discussing what actions I needed to take before the next meeting. Richard ended by giving me a copy of his Tutorial Record, which summarised the main points discussed in the tutorial, a diagram headed 'Starting to Research' and a copy of his handout 'Research Checklist Schedule' which he said I should use to help clarify my thinking and focus my research. The Schedule looks useful if a bit longwinded. But he did say that it was something I should work on over a period of time and update as my thinking evolves.

Overall the session went as well as I could have expected. After the first few minutes I was able to relax and listen to what Richard had to say and the use of the recorder was a really good idea. I've learnt so much from just listening to the tape again. But I don't like the sound of my voice.

Like most of the lecturers on the course Richard was really friendly and interested in what I was doing. I don't know why I thought he would be different. Maybe it's just his title, Research Supervisor. It sounds so formal. Anyway, now that I have broken the ice I might be a little more relaxed next time and perhaps think of a few questions to ask him.

Record of tutorial

Student: Sam Sylon   **Date: 15/9/XX**
SUMMARY OF KEY LEARNING POINTS

What is research about?

Research is not just about proving things or discovering new knowledge. It can be about exploring common everyday situations. It's a way of learning that involves the collection of data from other people and one of its purposes is to improve the researcher's professional knowledge and/or practice.

KIS – Keep it Simple. Don't be overambitious

A good piece of research needs to be self-contained and doable in the time available. Define the focus of your research in a statement no more than 200 words. Avoid collecting lots of data which you will never be able to use because of the word limit.

Research questions

Once you have a clear statement that describes your research identify four aspects of the issue that you particularly wish to explore. These will become your research questions. A good research question will be:

- clear, concise and focused;
- a sentence or so long;

➡

- of personal and professional interest;
- manageable in the time available.

One research question might be enough for a short project, two or three for a 5,000-word assignment and maybe four or five for a long project or dissertation over 10,000 words.

Agreed action points

Sam will:

- Complete the 'What' and 'Why' sections of the Research Checklist Schedule.
- Visit the library and look at how journal articles and dissertations are structured and written.

Starting to research

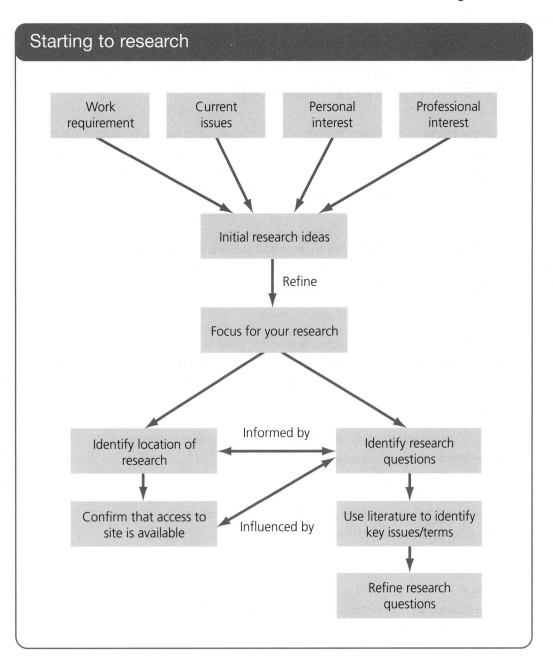

RESEARCH CHECKLIST SCHEDULE

Use the following questions to help you think about your research. Start each question on a new sheet of paper and provide as much detail as you can. You should amend and update the schedule as your ideas evolve and if required it can be used as the basis for your research proposal.

What?

Summarise in plain English the aims and objectives of your research. Write a short statement, between 100 and 200 words, that describes the focus of your research. List your research questions.

Why?

Why do you want to carry out this research? What is its purpose? Why it is worth doing? (Remember that research into a topic of professional interest will very often improve your professional knowledge and practice).

How?

How do you intend to carry out the research? Will you use interviews, observations or questionnaires?

Where?

Where will the research take place? Do you have access to this location? If you have to negotiate access, how long will it take?

When?

When will you conduct the research? How will you monitor your progress? Draft out a realistic timetable that allows for delays and use it to monitor your progress. The first entry on your timetable should be the date you have to hand the work in on. Work back from this date.

Ethics?

Have you obtained and read the British Educational Research Association (BERA) ethical guidelines free from **www.bera.ac.uk**. You will need to discuss the ethical issues raised by your research with your supervisor.

Impact?

What will be the impact of this research, on your pupils/students, school/college/university and/or your professional practice?

Additional information on the issues covered by this tutorial can be found at/in:

- www.pearsoned.co.uk/colesmcgrath
- Cohen, L., Mannion, L. and Morrison, K. (2007) *Research Methods in Education (6th ed.).* Routledge Falmer: London, Ch. 2.
- Newby, P. (2010) *Research Methods for Education.* Longman, Pearson: Harlow, Ch. 2.

HOW TO STRUCTURE YOUR RESEARCH REPORT

Aim of tutorial

To provide you with guidance on how to structure a research report and the content of each section. Some readers may find aspects of this tutorial challenging because it introduces jargon which is commonly used in the research process. If you find the tutorial heavy going we suggest you skim read it. This will provide you with an idea of what you are aiming to write. You can return to the tutorial later, for more detailed consideration, when you are more familiar with some of the terminology used. The glossary might help too.

Contents

→ Style of writing
→ The abstract
→ The introduction
→ The literature review
→ The research methodology
→ Findings and analysis
→ Conclusions

Sam's reflection

28 September

I was looking forward to my meeting with Richard. I'd done my homework and I had a number of queries that I wanted to raise with him.

Review of tutorial

When I entered, Richard was talking to a colleague on the phone about Albion's win at the weekend. He seemed in a good mood. He waved me into a chair and I sat down. These sessions were proving to be much more informal than I had expected.

'Sorry about that Sam,' he said, hanging up. 'How have you been?'

'Confused,' I said. 'I did what you asked and visited the library to look at how research reports and dissertations are structured but they seem to differ from report to report. Some of them are even written in the first person.'

'What's wrong with writing in the first person?'

'It doesn't sound very academic.'

'So you think a research report needs to be written in a formal academic style to be acceptable?'

'Well, yes.'

'Don't confuse good academic writing with formality, complexity and the use of long words. At times it seems to me as if some academics write in order to show how clever they are. Thankfully others write in order to communicate their ideas. I like the latter. Therefore, my advice is to avoid trying to write in an academic manner and instead write as clearly and unambiguously as you can. To help you do that I suggest that you never use a long word where a shorter one will do. In addition any sentence longer than 20 words is probably two sentences and unless you are a grammarian the longer a sentence is the more chance there is that you will get the grammar wrong. The current record for a sentence that I've marked is 168 words! That's a paragraph. There are many fewer grammatical errors in the tabloid newspapers than in the broadsheets, simply because they apply the KIS principle – Keep It Simple.'

'Similarly with paragraphs,' he continued. 'Each paragraph should only deal with one issue or point. This means that some paragraphs can be very short while others are much longer. As for writing in the first person, it's perfectly alright to write in the first person. It sounds far more natural to say "I found that . . .," rather than to say "The researcher found that" . . . but we can talk about this more when we discuss **quantitative** and **qualitative** approaches to research.'

'That sounds good to me,' I said.

Sam's reflection

28 September

What is this man on that he keeps a record of the longest sentence that has ever been submitted for him to mark? Get a life! Mind you I found what he had to say reassuring. I've found some of the writing, especially in the academic journals, difficult to understand. I suppose it's a bit like going to the gym. At first it is really hard but as you get fitter it becomes easier. I have to get my mind fit. Mind you it was nice to hear that I didn't have to write like that. What I need to do is write clearly and unambiguously and I can even write in the first person if I want to.

Review of tutorial

'So what's the proper way to structure a report?' I asked.

'OK,' he said. 'There are different ways that you can structure a research report and if you go to another university you should check out their house style, including how they feel about you writing in the first person. But broadly speaking there are certain key features that appear in all reports, regardless of what they might be called. So, let's start at the beginning. How important do you think the title is?'

That seemed an obvious question. 'Very important,' I replied.

'Why?'

'Because it needs to tell the reader what the research is about.'

'That's one view. But what if I told you that it wasn't very important?'

'I'd disagree with you.'

'OK, let's leave that for the moment. What follows the title?'

'A table of contents and a list of all the charts, tables and figures that you've used. Oh, and a list of any appendices.'

'Correct. And what follows that?'

'The introduction.'

'Before that?'

'Oh, you mean an abstract.'

'Exactly. Abstracts are hard to write and I suggest that you leave yours until you have finished writing up your research. The abstract needs to summarise in about 200 words what the research is about and what the key issues and findings are. It is not something that you can dash off in 10 minutes. A good abstract can take several days to write.'

'But I can't afford to spend days writing 200 words,' I said louder than I'd intended.

'I didn't say that you had to work on it eight hours a day. What I meant was that you need to write and rewrite your abstract over a period of about an hour. Then put it in a drawer and forget about it for a few days, then take it out. Read it again and make any changes that you think are required. Then repeat the process until your abstract presents an accurate summation of your research.'

'So what you're saying is that I need to reflect on what I've written and change it as required.'

'That's it. Then it's the introduction. So what are you going to write about in the introduction?'

'Well, I suppose I explain what the research is about.'

'Precisely. You write your focal paragraph. We touched on that last time. Have you written your focal paragraph and revised your research questions?'

I gave him what I had completed and he spent a couple of minutes reading it and writing comments in the margin.

'This is pretty good,' he said. 'Your focus is sharper than it was and you've clearly decided that what you're interested in is the children's own view of their safety and not those of teachers or parents. This has the advantage of providing a sharper focus for your research which means that you can spend more time analysing the data you collect. You can also dig deeper into it because you have less data to analyse. Your focal paragraph makes it clear to the reader what the work is going to be about. Well done.'

'What about my research questions?'

'They're a lot better. You've got rid of the question marks and they are clear and unambiguous.'

Sam's reflection

28 September

I felt relieved when he said the focal paragraph and research questions were ok. I'd put a lot of effort into them. I certainly think that the changes I made capture more clearly what I want to do and most importantly I think it's going to be easier. Because now I'm exploring attitudes and not trying to prove what the attitudes are.

Review of tutorial

'So now you have an abstract, a focal paragraph and your research questions. What do they do?'

'Oh, I know where this is going. You're going to tell me that because I have outlined what my research is about in both the abstract and the introduction my title doesn't have to do that job.'

'Correct. People spend too much time worrying about titles. Keep it short and relevant but don't try and summarise your entire research project in the title. I once had an MA student whose dissertation title was half a page long.' He grimaced at the memory, before continuing. 'Now having said what you're going to research, you need to explain to the reader why you're interested in the subject. Why it's worth doing. Usually it will be because it's of professional interest and will help you to improve your professional practice. However, it might just be a subject that has always fascinated you. So you need to write another paragraph or two explaining your motivation.'

'What if I'm only doing it to pass the exam?'

'Then I suggest you're economical with the truth,' he said smiling.

'You mean lie?'

'I couldn't possibly say that.'

I grinned and moved on. 'What else needs to go in the introduction?'

'You need to do what all good teachers do. In every lesson, you tell your students what you are going to cover in the session, you cover it and then you tell them what you've covered. It's the same with your report. Very briefly, you outline the remaining contents of the report. For example: In the Literature Review I explore the literature that relates to children's perception of safety at school. The **Research Methodology** section outlines the reasons why I have adopted a qualitative approach and used questionnaires as my primary data collection tool. The Findings contains a description and analysis of the data I have collected and the Conclusion identifies what I have learnt from the research, discusses any weaknesses in what I've done and details areas for further study.'

'Hang on, are you saying I should point out the weaknesses of my research in the conclusions?' I asked surprised. 'Won't that reduce my mark?'

'No it's good practice. No piece of research is perfect. What you need to demonstrate is that you are aware of how your work could be improved. That sort of critical self-reflection will gain points not lose them.'

Sam's reflection

29 September

Thinking about it I realise that most of the examples I've looked at followed the format suggested by my supervisor. They did have an abstract and the introduction did set out what the report was about and what the purpose of the research was. However, not all of them explained the layout of the rest of the work. I think they should have. After all it does help the reader to know what's coming next and to skip it if they want to. But I'm not so sure about revealing the weaknesses in my research. I'll have to think about that a bit more.

Review of tutorial

'OK,' I said, 'So then it's the literature review?'

'That's right. Now we'll have a full tutorial devoted just to literature review, so for now we will just do a quick overview. What goes into a literature review?'

'Anything that you've read that is relevant to your study,' I said confidently.

'No. That is not a good idea. As you progress up the academic ladder, you'll learn more and more about whatever it is that you're studying. Very soon the word limit for the assignment will stop you from saying everything you know about the topic. That's why you have to be selective and only include material which is relevant and up to date. In addition, where there's more than one side to an argument you need to report the differing views. It's essential that you **evaluate** the literature and that you don't just accept what one writer says.'

'Won't giving all sides of the argument use up a lot of words?'

'Not if you're selective and avoid using long quotes. Try to summarise the arguments in your own words and do remember to reference the source of the ideas. Use short powerful quotes to emphasise a particular point that you want to make. If you're really good you can take the arguments of two or more writers and **synthesise** what they say on a particular subject.'

'What do you mean by synthesise. Is it the same as analyse?'

'When you were a child did you ever play with Lego bricks?'

I nodded yes.

'Me too, and when you became bored with the house you built you took it apart?'

'Yes.'

'Well that is analysis. You take an argument, some data or a theory, and you take it apart brick by brick. Synthesis occurs when you take the same bricks and build something new. What was a house now becomes a stable or an aeroplane. You can do the same with theories, you can take two or more theories, take them apart and then reassemble them into a new or revised theory.'

'That can't be easy.'

'No it isn't but if you can do it you will score well in any piece of academic writing.'

'So in the literature review I need to select the most appropriate literature that deals with research topic. But how do I check that it's appropriate?'

'Easy. Firstly, except for seminal or really important books and articles only use literature that has been published in the last five or six years.'

'If I do that won't I miss out lots of important writers?'

'I'm not saying you can't use older references but use them sparingly. It's true that the latest writing often summarises what previous writers have had to say on a subject and that can be useful. However, world renowned writers have got there because of the power of their message and it can be really revealing to read the original work.'

'OK.'

'Secondly either use the literature or lose it! What I mean by that is the literature review is there to help you understand and analyse your findings. So if you don't use a reference in your findings you need to ask yourself, why have I discussed it in the literature review? The theories and ideas contained in the literature review are there to help you explain, explore, confound or support your findings. That's one of the purposes of the literature review. Having said that, there's one type of literature that you may need but which you may not refer to in your findings. What do you think it is?'

I must have looked blank because after a short pause Richard said 'Background information. That's information which contextualises the issues. For example you might want to briefly outline government policy on an issue before you get to grips with it in your institution.'

29 September

What Richard said about the literature review seemed to make sense. But I still suspect that I'll collect far more literature than I can use. If I'm not careful the literature review will be huge. It looks like I'm going to have to learn to edit my work. But what if I cut something out by mistake? I'd better think about how I'm going to save different drafts on the computer.

Nor do I feel comfortable criticising the work of published authors. After all they're the experts. How am I supposed to criticise them? Maybe the easiest way for me to do this is to compare and contrast what different writers have to say on the same subject.

Review of tutorial

'OK. What's next?' I asked.

'It's the research methodology section. Now this is crucial to any piece of research. In it you have to demonstrate that you're a competent researcher and that you understand a range of research methodologies, data collection tools and issues associated with carrying out research.'

'So it's a practical section where I describe what I've done?'

'Partially. You'll need to outline what you've done but you'll also have to justify your choice of methodology and methods and to do that you need to understand some research theory. Again, we'll look at this in detail in future sessions, but basically I suggest that you start the section with a summary statement such as: the research methodology that I adopted was mainly **qualitative** in nature, the research strategy was that of a **case study**, the methods used to collect data included observation, **questionnaires** and semi-structured **interviews**.'

I must have appeared confused because without waiting for me to say anything Richard continued speaking 'What you need to do is define each of the words or phrases that I emphasised and discuss their strengths and weaknesses. For example, define what qualitative research is and explain why you've adopted a largely qualitative approach.'

'But what if I don't want to do qualitative research, whatever that is?'

'I'm sorry, I haven't made myself clear. I'm not suggesting for a moment that you have to use these precise methodologies, strategies and data collection methods. It's just a format that you can use to start the methodology chapter. Like a maths formula, you can drop anything into the place where I've emphasised certain words. Don't worry about the terms at the moment, you don't have to decide on what approach you're going to take until later.'

Sam's reflection

30 September

I remember thinking at the time that it was alright for him to say 'don't worry', but my head was ready to explode. I was hanging on by my fingertips. But I had consoled myself with the thought that it would all become clear when I've had a chance to review his notes and listen to the tape. If Dr. Reed sensed my confusion there was no sign of it. For with only a slight pause he launched into the next section. I must stop him doing this in future. If I don't understand something I must ask him to go over it again.

Review of tutorial

'Then you need to write a paragraph on bias, triangulation, validity, reliability, the analysis of data and ethics. We'll discuss what each of these terms means later but you may want to look them up in a good textbook before then.'

Grasping at straws and trying to slow down the delivery of information, I asked, 'Is there any textbook that you would recommend?'

'What suits one person very often doesn't suit another. The best thing to do is to visit the library, or a good academic bookshop and have a look at the various textbooks on research. There is nothing like handling the text, flicking thought the pages and reading extracts for finding one that suits you. It is also useful to use at least two different texts because ...'

'You should never just take one person's viewpoint,' I said.

'Exactly.'

'OK, I'll visit the library and check out what they have. I need to have a look at what journals they have.'

'Good idea. Once you have dealt with the theory surrounding your research approach you need to briefly outline what you did and the order in which you did it. This can be done in the form of a table if you are short of space. Make sure that the theory matches the practice. For example if you said that you were going to use interviews your description needs to talk about interviews and not questionnaires!'

Sam's reflection

30 September

As I'm writing up these notes I'm starting to realise that what Richard was giving me was a framework for how to lay out a research methodology chapter. The details about what goes into each part will come later. For now I don't have to worry about what the terms mean. It's enough to know that there's a template that I can use. In many ➡

ways the summary statement at the start of the research methodology chapter is like my introduction at the start of the lesson. It summarises what will be discussed in the chapter. But it also acts as a kind of checklist reminding me of the issues that I must cover.

Review of tutorial

'Then it's the findings.'

At last, I thought, 'something that isn't technical'.

'The findings and conclusion sections are the crux of any research assignment. They represent the creative element of your work and as such they should account for a minimum of 50 per cent of the work.'

'So how's the other 50 per cent divided up?'

'Good question. I'd use about 5 per cent for the abstract and introduction, 25 per cent in the literature review and 20 per cent for the research methodology, 40 per cent for the findings and 10 per cent for the conclusions. These are a guideline and your research may differ. But if you find that only 20 per cent of your assignment is given over to the findings and conclusions there's probably something wrong with it.'

Sam's reflection

31 September

At the time I didn't think much about what Richard had said but on reflection it's actually very useful. Not only does it provide guidance on how much goes in each section it also enables me to break the task down into small chunks. Instead of a 7500 word assignment I now have six mini tasks, the longest of which is about 2000 words. That makes life easier. I can manage that.

Review of tutorial

'Is there any particular way that I should write up or organise my findings?'

'A lot depends on what your findings are. When you've collected some data we can discuss how best to report the findings. But essentially what you need to do is to introduce the chapter by briefly explaining the scope and content of the section.'

'Oh, we're back to telling them what you are going to teach them, tell them and tell them what you have taught them,' I said, feeling pleased with my understanding.'

'Exactly. You then need to take each of your findings and analyse them. Remember to use your literature review to do this. So for example "As Parker (20xx) predicted I found that ..." or, conversely, "In contrast to Parker (20xx) I found no evidence for his claim that ..."'

'So what you're saying is that I have a conversation with the literature.'

'Precisely, you use it to explain, explore, support and challenge your findings.'

'But what about my own analysis? Doesn't that count for anything?'

'Indeed it does. However, you must support your interpretation by reference to the literature or the data you've collected. You can argue a case for a particular interpretation of the data but it must be both reasonable and logical. Otherwise it is just your opinion. And that's not worth much in an academic paper, although it might make you a living as a journalist, where the facts are seldom allowed to get in the way of a good story – or the story the reporter wants to sell.'

'That sounds cynical.'

'Maybe. But remember,' he said smiling, 'a cynic is just a disappointed romantic. Besides, academic writing is about arguing a case and supporting it with evidence not opinion. It is good practice to follow Hayek's advice and present the strongest argument you can against your own views and then demonstrate why your arguments are superior.'

'That sounds like a lot of work.'

'It is, but it's also what distinguishes good academic work from the average.'

It sounded as if Richard felt strongly about this issue and my time was running out so I changed the subject, asking 'Is there anything else I need to do in the findings?'

'Yes. Reference all material correctly. If you don't already have the guide to referencing from the library pick up a copy while you are over there. We use the Harvard System here but you may be used to a different system. Every college or university will have a particular model and it's important to know which system is in use and to follow it.'

'But why's it so important?'

'There are a number of reasons. Firstly it helps you to avoid plagiarism. If you don't acknowledge where you got an idea or a quote from you could be accused of passing off someone else's work as your own. That is probably the greatest sin that an academic can commit. Secondly, when marking your work I might want to follow up an idea that you are writing about. Without a reference I wouldn't know where to start.'

'But why would you want to follow up an idea of mine?'

'It may be new to me or perhaps I think that you have misquoted or misunderstood what the writer said and I want to check up on it. Thirdly, good referencing is a sort of quality guarantee. If you reference material carefully, the chances are that you'll also have been careful with other aspects of the work, while poor referencing might indicate that you've been equally slapdash in the conduct of your research.'

'So I need to get it right?'

'Absolutely. You'll seldom fail an assignment because of poor referencing alone but you will lose marks.'

'What then?'

He checked his watch and said, 'The last part of the report is the conclusion. It is essential that your conclusions flow naturally from your findings, so make sure that there's coherence between what you say in the findings and what you discuss in the conclusion. You would be surprised how often the two don't match up. In the conclusion you talk about what you have learnt as a result of carrying out the research. It won't be possible to cover everything so pick out the main lessons that you have learned from the exercise.'

'What about recommendations, are they the same as conclusions?'

'No. Conclusions are discursive. Having carried out your research you discuss what you have learnt. Recommendations are far more directive. With a recommendation, you indicate what action you want the reader to take. For example, you might write: "It is recommended that two teachers always be on playground duty during the lunch hour at any one time." It's quite common for research projects to only have conclusions but occasionally people may want to make recommendations.'

'Anything else?'

'No new literature or findings can be introduced at this stage. You should only comment on what you've written about in the previous pages. You should also comment on any weaknesses in the research and identify areas that require additional research.'

'Oh we're back to highlighting my mistakes?' I said, knowing that it would get a reaction from him.

'No it is not like that. It is about you critically evaluating the quality of research. That is an essential skill for any researcher. No piece of research is perfect. There will always be ways in which it could be improved. Besides, anyone marking a piece of research will want to see that you're able to critique your own work. Far from losing you marks it is likely to improve your score. Remember that this sort of project is as much about learning about the research process as about answering questions.'

Sam's reflection

31 September

We seemed to cover a lot in the session but now that I've had the time to go over the transcript twice I can see that there is a lot of useful information in it. There are obviously different ways of writing up research but it's essential to include all the main elements (abstract, introduction, literature review, research methodology, findings, which includes analysis, and conclusions). What Richard has provided me with is a template that I can fit my data into and embellish it with subheadings as required.

Record of tutorial

Student: Sam Sylon   **Date: 28/9/XX**
SUMMARY OF KEY LEARNING POINTS

The following elements are required in a research report.

Title Page

Table of contents

List of figures and tables

List of appendices

Abstract (Approximately 200 words)

Introduction (Approximately 5 per cent of word count)

- Define the question or scope of the topic that you are writing about.
- Outline your setting and role within it.
- Explain why you are interested in this particular topic and justify why it is worth investigating.
- Outline the remaining content of the assignment.

Review of literature (Approximately 25 per cent of word count)

- Introduce the section by briefly explaining the scope and content.
- Remember that this is a critical review of the literature and not just repetition of previous work. Set competing views on a topic against each other – compare and contrast them.
- Reference material correctly – see Student's Handbook and/or the Information Services guide to writing references.
- Avoid using excessively long quotes. Only quote if the form of words is critical to the message. A summary of the writer's opinions in your own words is more valuable than a long quote – anyone can copy from a book.
- Avoid plagiarism at all costs.
- Check that the material is relevant. If it's not used to explain/explore your findings why include it?

Research methodology (Approximately 20 per cent of word count)
The research methodology section is a crucial element of your assignment and one that people can struggle with. This summary suggests one way that this section can be structured, but it is not the only way!

- Start with a summary of the research approach that has been adopted, e.g. The research methodology was **qualitative** in nature, the research strategy was that of a **case study**, the methods used to collect data included **observation, questionnaires** and **semi-structured interviews**.

- Define what is meant by each of the words in bold above and discuss the strengths and weaknesses associated with that approach, strategy or method. Explain how you have addressed the following:

  - Bias

  - Triangulation

  - Validity and reliability

  - The analysis of data

  - Ethics

- Describe what you actually did. Remember that this a vital part of the methodology. Someone should be able to repeat your research from the information that you give. Then provide a timeline to guide the reader through the process.

- Provide a short conclusion that considers the strengths and weaknesses of the approach taken in the light of experience and what might be done differently if the research were repeated.

Findings (Approximately 40 per cent of the word count)

- Introduce the section by briefly explaining its scope and content.

- Discuss one point at a time and link the various issues to be discussed with linking phrases such as 'In the above section I considered the motivational impact of transformational leadership. In this section I shall explore how transformational leadership can be employed to exploit staff.' Use linking words and phrases such as 'conversely' and 'in contrast with'.

- Link findings back to issues discussed in the literature review, e.g. 'As Grayson (20xx) predicted I found that . . .'
- Reference all material correctly.

Conclusions (Approximately 10 per cent of the word count)

- It is essential that conclusions flow naturally from the findings.
- No new literature or findings should be introduced at this stage.
- Comment on any areas of weakness in the assignment or areas that might require additional research. The 'rule of three' is useful: Outline the three most important findings from the research.

List of references

Appendices

Agreed action points

Sam will:

- **Speak to the librarian and identify the full range of resources, paper-based and electronic, that are available to students and their location.**
- **Check out what journals are available in the library and online.**
- **Obtain and read a copy of the library guide to referencing.**

The research report

Introduction

What is the focus of your research?

What do you want to find out and why?

Literature review

What have others said about your subject/critical evaluation?

Methodology

Data collection/validity/ reliability/bias/ethics/analytical methods.

Findings

Report, present, explore and analyse your data using your literature review.

Research report

Explain in a clear and logical manner using plain English your research journey. Include in the final report:

- Abstract
- Introduction
- Literature review
- Research methodology
- Findings and analysis
- Conclusion
- References
- Appendices

Conclusions

What were the most significant issues identified by your research?

How did the research process/findings impact on your professional practice?

Handout

PRESENTATION OF RESEARCH REPORT

What follows is some general advice on how to ensure that your assignment is well presented, clear and logical.

- Check what the course requirements are as regards font size and spacing. This is normally size 12 double spaced. Use size 16 bold for main headings and 14 bold for subheadings.
- Use subheadings within chapters to organise your material.
- Use bullet points in moderation.
- Carry out a spell and grammar check of your work prior to final submission. A red wavy line means that a correction is required and a green line indicates that you need to review the grammar.
- Ensure that your work is logically structured and not haphazard. If you find that your work jumps from issue to issue and back again it is likely that your structure is weak. Planning is vital here. Consider flow charts or mind maps.
- Never use a word or phrase the meaning of which you are unsure. If in doubt use a dictionary.
- Never discuss a theory that you don't fully understand.
- Check that you have no sentence longer than 20 words. If you do you probably have two or more sentences.
- Only one issue should be discussed in a single paragraph. Remember: one point = one paragraph.
- Keep it simple. Good academic work is all about discussing complex ideas in a simple and clear manner.

Additional information on the issues covered by this tutorial can be found at/in:

- www.pearsoned.co.uk/colesmcgrath
- Denscombe, M. (2008) *The Good Research Guide (3rd ed.). McGraw Hill*: Maidenhead, Ch. 15.
- Newby, P. (2010) *Research Methods for Education*. Longman, Pearson: Harlow, Ch. 14.

WRITING YOUR LITERATURE REVIEW

Aim of tutorial

To introduce you to the notion of a conceptual framework. Specifically it provides guidance on how to find and evaluate relevant literature, structure and write up your literature review.

Contents

→ Starting a literature search

→ How reliable are the sources of literature?

→ Two ways to structure a literature review

→ Searching electronically for literature

→ How to recognise bias

→ Keeping track of literature read

Sam's reflection

11 October

From what I've heard the literature review sounds difficult. In the last tutorial we started to discuss how to find literature on theories relevant to my project. So I need to be clear about what the focus of my research is and the theories that relate to it.

My project is about safety, so I need to define what I mean by safety as I think that this will help me decide on the main areas for my literature review. Richard mentioned the idea of 'seminal' documents. These are ones which have had a big influence on thinking in a particular area. The book by Lowe (found on first visit to the library by wandering around and looking at what was on the shelves. How lucky was that?) seems interesting. He discusses the main aspects of child safety which seems like a good area for me to focus on. I like the idea of seminal documents – this has been a great help. I suppose the 'Every Child Matters' report would be another. I'll have a chat with Richard about this.

Review of tutorial

Richard was all business when I entered. As soon as he had finished saying hello he said '**Right, so it's the literature review now?**' He probably had an appointment after me.

'Hmm, I think that this is going to be the worst part of my project.'

'**No, it's fascinating. It's when you start to uncover the different perspectives on a topic. You often find that it's much more involved than you thought. I suggested that you have a browse in the library, so did you find anything?**'

'Yes, I found a book by someone called Lowe. It seemed to cover a lot of what I was interested in, but it was published in 1997. Does that matter?'

'No. He probably published more after that and there may be another edition. The main thing is that it opens the door to literature relevant to your topic. Now you can start to search for publications in a similar area. Hopefully you'll have found some new key words to use for your searches and you'll have an idea of the concepts involved.'

'The book certainly helped me identify the issues. Lowe says there are four main aspects of safety, physical, environmental, social and cognitive. Could I structure my research around these areas?'

'Indeed you could. The two most common ways to structure a literature review is chronologically, meaning you discuss the literature in the order in which it was published and thematically. I often suggest that research questions are used as subheadings in both the literature review and the findings. In that way the topic is automatically broken down into manageable sections. This also makes it easier to have that all-important dialogue between the literature and the findings when you're trying to analyse the data.'

'I like the sound of that. My findings could be organised as a mirror image of my literature review.'

'Indeed it could. But let's not jump the gun. You've got your **conceptual framework** and some useful key words. What you need to do now is to start your literature search. Remember that you need to aim for diverse sources. You already have one book and you'll be familiar with *Every Child Matters*, the Children's Act, 2004 and the "Every Child Matters: Change for Children" paper.'

I nodded yes.

'Government reports are often really useful as they sometimes change policy. For you the government report into the death of Victoria Climbié might be relevant. It's also a good idea to look at selected websites such as the DCSF, OFSTED and NfER, for example, as they will almost certainly have published reports on relevant topics. Then there are periodicals such as professional magazines, *The Times Educational Supplement*, union publications and those from subject associations. These are all sources of useful information. Once you've looked at these, you can begin your electronic search for reviews and journal articles.'

'But won't I have enough already?' I said pleadingly as a vision of drowning in paper crowded into my mind.

'Hopefully the documents that we've discussed will be critical, but they don't always compare and contrast different views. For that you need a wider range of writers. Remember that critical appraisal is a very important aspect of working at this level. The point about academic journals is that they'll help you to develop your critical skills. They'll often promote a particular viewpoint, but this should be supported by appropriate evidence. Your task will be to consider whether you think that the evidence supports that viewpoint or not.'

'I'm not sure that I can do that. I mean, how do I know who to believe?'

'It's not so much "who to believe", but whether you think that the evidence supports the judgements made by the writer. There are a few tricks here to help you. You can consider the provenance of the authors and the source.'

'What do you mean by provenance?'

'Provenance means the origins, but in this case it's a bit more than that. If you take information from a website, how do you know whether the person producing the webpage has sufficient experience to come to a valid viewpoint?'

'I don't. But academic papers are reviewed by other academics, so I should be able to trust them more than websites shouldn't I?'

'Probably. But it's a judgement you have to make. However, there is a hierarchy of journals. Some publishers have better reputations than others. You can't be expected to know that now, but this expertise will develop in time. Certainly most journals in college and university libraries are a reasonable bet because someone has had to justify their purchase. Here, you can have this handout in which I have ranked the sources of literature in order of how reliable they are.' (See page 54.)

'There's a lot here. Do I have to use one example from each source?'

'No, not at all. It's just a list of the sources that you might use. When deciding how much you can rely on what someone is saying you might also want to look at the methodology described in the paper and decide whether you think it was valid and reliable. We'll look at what these words mean in Tutorial 4. So where are you going to start your search?'

'I thought that I'd Google my key words and identify some more sources?'

'Well, that's not a bad idea. However, I would recommend Google Scholar because it focuses on academic and peer reviewed sources and includes abstracts. The great thing is that the articles are ranked by the number of citations each has attracted, so you tend to get the most popular ones first. You can even click on "Cited by" and see all the documents citing a particular source.'

'Ah, now I see why it wasn't so important that my first reference was 1997. If someone has cited that book, then they're likely to be working in a similar area and to have published later, so it's a way of tracing more modern works.'

'Exactly. It's also worth mentioning Web of Science and the Arts & Humanities Citation index. These are electronic citation indexes usually available in most university libraries. You can enter a publication and they give you a list of publications citing your original source. There are also specialist search engines such as the British Education Index and the British Humanities Index. Some websites provide subject specialist links too like "Socioweb" and "Intut". I also like "Zetoc", which lists the contents pages of most journals. It's an easy way keep up to date on what's being published. It's always worth checking the electronic resources available in the library. Just go and have a play. You will be amazed at what you find.'

'The power of the Net. What about just going to the library and physically looking at the education journals?'

'Actually that's a very good idea. Once you know the subject area that you're interested in it only takes a couple of hours to have a quick look at all the relevant journals in the library and identify which ones cover your specific interests. Once you've identified which are useful you can go through the contents page of each edition and identify any relevant articles.'

'How far back should I go?'

'If you go back five years you will very quickly identify any seminal books or journals that were published earlier and if need be you can consult them.'

'A colleague told me that what he did was find one really good article and then he used the list of references at the back to trace other relevant books and articles and then used their lists of references to expand his search.'

'You can do that but writers very often reference other writers who agree with their own views and arguments. What does that do for your literature review?'

'Makes it unbalanced?'

'It makes it biased. So you can use a manual search but you need to guard against author bias.'

'I thought the literature search would be straightforward. But it seems a lot more complicated than I'd anticipated.'

'Don't worry about it. There is no perfect way to do a literature search. Most students use a mixture of wandering around the library with purpose and using the various electronic search engines that are available. And the most important word in that sentence is "purpose". It really is a question of deciding what you need, then choosing the most appropriate method of searching.'

'But I could miss a vital article.'

'Actually that's unlikely. If you read four or five relevant articles that are up to date, they will probably list 80 plus references between them. Any seminal work in your area is very likely to be in that list. It's like Gary Player the golfer used to say, "the harder you work, the luckier you get." It's the same with you. The more you search the better your literature review will be.'

Sam's reflection

11 October

Who the hell is Gary Player?

Help! I'm drowning in literature. There's an awful lot of stuff out there that I need to be aware of and I can't read it all or use it all in my project. Stay calm. At least now I've an idea where to look. With so much to plough through I can see why it's so important to clarify my concepts at the start. The correct key words and combination of words will limit the amount of material that I have to look at.

Review of tutorial

'I'll have to find somewhere to keep all this paperwork so that I can find what I need when it comes to summarising the information and writing my literature review,' I said.

'Well there are a few tricks that might help. You should write the literature review as you do your research. Don't wait until the end to start writing. That way what you write will feed into the planning of your research and the analysis of results. So do it a bit at a time. I know that the literature review seems like a daunting task, but you don't need to summarise the whole article or book. You just need to summarise what's relevant to your studies.'

'But how do I know what's relevant?' I asked despairingly.

'You need to keep referring back to the focus of your research, your research questions and key words. It helps to break it down by starting with subheadings relating to your individual themes – for example physical aspects of safety – you can then file your resources under these categories. It really helps if you keep a record of each reference and a brief summary of what it contains. You can use a database such as Access or specialist software such as EndNote – we'll talk about this later – or just old-fashioned index cards.'

'It sounds good in theory but I'm still not convinced. Potentially I have a mountain of literature to read and I don't really know where to start.'

'Selective reading is the key. It's a good idea to consider what you want to get out of a source before you read it and make a list of points. You'll find that similar points relate to several sources, so you don't need to do this for each one. Now read the part of the document that is relevant to what you need to know. Think of the sections that you often find in a research paper for example. How could you use these for selective reading?'

'I suppose the abstract would tell me whether the source is worth reading at all; maybe the introduction would do that too. The literature review would cover the concepts if that was what I was after. It seems like cheating, but I could read the conclusions and skip the rest!'

'Indeed you could. You could also use the subheadings and skip those that seem irrelevant. The problem is that you can't always be sure what is irrelevant, so try skimming through some sections and reading others more carefully. Check to see if the report has an executive summary, if so read that first.'

'You sound just like the trainer I had on my speed reading course. She said that we have to read strategically and that we need to develop a range of reading strategies including skimming, reading just the introduction and conclusion and just checking for key words and phrases. Then if we decide it is important we can read the document more carefully.'

'She was right. But once you do identify important information remember to highlight it. You can do this with a highlighter pen on hard copies but you can also do it electronically. But remember to use different colours, that way you can colour-code different themes.'

'I hadn't thought of that,' I said.

'You can even copy selected quotes directly into your literature review file, but be very careful and use a different font colour so that you don't include someone else's work as your own accidentally. Remember . . .'

'Avoid plagiarism at all costs,' I said.

Richard smiled and nodded. 'That's another reason why it is vital to record each reference accurately, particularly the page number in the case of quotes. Remember to only quote when the form of words is such that the meaning would be changed if you put it any other way; otherwise paraphrase.'

'Can you give me an example of what you mean?'

He was silent for moment thinking and then lent forward. 'OK,' he said, 'Jimi Hendrix is alleged to have said "Knowledge speaks, but wisdom listens". It's a great quote. It's short, sharp and powerful. It would be impossible to paraphrase it without losing impact. So you would use the quote as it is. However, faced with a page of government prose you could probably summarise it in your own words and lose none of the meaning. Just remember that if you use a long quote all you've done is prove that you can copy. If you summarise the information in your own words accurately you're demonstrating that you understand what's been said. But sometimes you need a quote because it captures in a forceful way exactly what you want to say. Which brings us back to Jimi, are you a fan?'

Sam's reflection

11 October

I thought it was best not to tell him that Jimi was my father's generation and side-stepped his enquiry. I wonder if he plays air guitar to 'All along the watchtower'? Now there is a image that I don't need in my head.

I'd been worried that I'd have to read loads of material and then sift through it again when it came to writing the literature review. Luckily, Richard's suggestion that I summarise as I go should eliminate the need to read everything twice. I must remember to note down the full reference of any book or article that I intend to use.

But wait, I've just had a ping moment with light bulbs flashing. If I have my sources gathered in files – paper and/or electronic – under themes relating to my research and I have highlighted all the important points. (I must be selective here and not highlight everything or I'll never see the wood for the trees) I can start to write about each theme by just reading my colour-coded text.

I should begin by trying to organise my sources into a logical order, but I can always move text around, so maybe it's not so important to get the order right at the beginning especially as I may need to include new themes as a result of my reading, or even delete some. Besides there's always my old friend 'cut and paste' to help me. Later I can add quotes, but only if I feel that they're really relevant and add impact to what I'm saying.

Review of tutorial

'Of course all you've done so far is describe what's in the literature; you must also evaluate it critically.'

'I guessed that was coming. Just as I thought that I'd cracked it, there's more to do. I hope that you've got an answer to that one too!'

'I don't pretend to have all the answers Sam. I'm really just describing an approach that works for some people. You may need to adapt it according to your style of working. A cheese is best eaten when mature and the critical approach is best taken when you have had a chance to reflect on your writing for a week or so.'

Where the heck did cheeses come from, I thought

'So after you have had a break from your literature I suggest that you re-read what you've written and make a note of the various views about each issue. Reference each view with the author's name. Then look at your notes and organise similar views together. You can now go back to your quite descriptive account and add phrases like: "x agrees with y on this issue because . . ." but "in contrast, z took a different view namely . . ."'

That way you can support your statements with the evidence from the source. This might seem long-winded, but you'll soon get used to it – it's just like playing the guitar – it comes with practice and it's a great skill to have. Basically you compare and contrast what different writers have to say.'

Sam's reflection

11 October

I was afraid he was going to start talking about Jimi again. Thankfully he didn't. But what he said does make me feel a bit better. I can see now how the task can be made manageable by breaking it down into individual tasks. I still feel that I need some way of having an overview. Another ping moment, I must be on a roll, I'll record my literature review on an A3 size mind map. That way I can keep track of what I do and see the links between different parts of the literature review. Maybe this would be useful for other sections too? I might ask Richard about this next time.

Right now I'm off to bed. I can listen to the next section of the tape tomorrow.

15 October

So much for listening to the tape the next day. Claire was off sick and I had to cover her classes for the last three days. Talk about panic. What with trying to plan her lessons and get the resources organised I barely had time to turn around. At busy times like this it helps to just do a bit each day or two, even if it's only 15 minutes. That way I keep the momentum going. Still, back to normal now.

Review of tutorial

'Now we need to talk a bit more about referencing. Can you remember why referencing is important?'

'You gave me three reasons last time. Firstly, it helps you to avoid charges of plagiarism. Secondly, the reader can follow up any of your references if they're interested or think that you've misrepresented the text. Thirdly, you said that it gave the reader confidence in what you'd written. Because if your referencing was done correctly then it would be likely that you'd also been careful with how you evaluated the literature and wrote up your findings,' I said feeling pleased that I'd checked my notes the night before.

'Very good! You're right about plagiarism. It's easy to accidentally include material from another author, so it's important to re-read your work. Markers are very experienced at recognising a change of "voice" in a piece of work and they will often Google a sentence to see if has been copied. It's also possible that your work will be checked using anti-plagiarism software. So guard against innocent plagiarism. We do find that some students think that it's honouring authors to copy their work into the assignment, but that doesn't show any criticality at all, it's just copying. OK, it sounds as if we can leave referencing . . .'

'Hang on. I have a few questions.' Richard nodded for me to continue. 'I'm not at all sure how often I need to reference. For example, if I use the same source several times in a paragraph, do I need to reference it every time?'

'There's no fixed rule here. If it's clear from your writing that you're still discussing a particular source, then you don't need to reference it again. If desperate you can use *ibid* – literally this means "the same place" – which means that the points under discussion come from the previously cited source. But don't use this too often as it can become tiresome to read.'

'Suppose the author I'm reading refers to someone else's work and ideas. If I want to refer to those how do I reference that material?'

'It's good practice to only cite sources that you have actually read in the original. When we find students referencing a source that they haven't read in the original we say that they have cited "indirectly". It's not a great problem if it only happens on the odd occasion, but if you do it repeatedly it becomes an issue of academic integrity because you're implying that you've read something when you haven't.

One way round this is to use "cited in" in your reference, where you quote the original source and say that this was cited in the source that you have read. For example, Banner cited in Benjamin and Grimm (20xx), the reference relates to Benjamin and Grimm's work. But if you do this too often it gives the impression that you're lazy and couldn't be bothered to read the original source.'

'OK, I accept that referencing is important but I did find it annoying recently when a tutor made a load of comments about my use of first names and book titles in the text.'

'Following the conventions of referencing is important because people have an expectation that something will be done in a particular way and if it's not, confusion can result. For example it is really difficult for someone else to follow up your work if the references are incorrect. And it can affect the readability of your work if your argument is interrupted by too much detail like first names or titles of articles.'

'So it's really all about good academic manners?'

'Correct! When it comes to the style of referencing, most universities have their own preferred approach and you must stick to it. This university uses the Harvard System, which is author and date in the text and the author/s family name and initials, date of publication, title, and details of publishers and place of publication in a list at the end. This list is always in alphabetical order by author's name. If there's more than one publication by an author, they go in chronological order. If there are two or more publications by the same author in the same year then you use "a", "b" etcetera to differentiate the texts. In the text you can quote up to two authors for a single source, e.g. Banner and Bruce (20xx), but if there are more than two authors, then you name the first one followed by "*et al*", which means "and others". Most people aren't too fussy about details such as whether you use commas after names or pg or p for "page", but the important thing is to be consistent. Anyway, all the details are in the library guide to referencing so go get a copy and read it.'

'I've picked up a copy already.'

'Good.'

'It said that bibliographies and footnotes shouldn't be used. Why is that?'

'Again these conventions differ from one university to another, so it's always worth checking. A bibliography is a list of sources that you've consulted, but not taken specific information from. Some universities, like ours, prefer that you only list those sources that you have cited in your work. Footnotes aren't used in the Harvard System and besides they interrupt the narrative flow and if a point is worth making it is worth making in the main body of the report.'

'Are there any computer packages that will help me do my references?'

'There are several. For example EndNote. This is an example of a bibliographic package. It's designed to help you store, summarise and integrate your references in your writing. But you could just keep an electronic list or even a database using Access or Excel. However, EndNote is designed for the purpose and you can present your references in any chosen format. You can get student versions, but it takes time to master. So if you're only managing a small number of references a manual system on index cards will be sufficient. However, if you have 50 plus references and you are intending to continue researching it is worth learning how to use a package.'

'OK. What about indenting quotes?'

'Again, convention varies and the rules aren't too strict on this, but short quotes of under 30 words can be included in the text in quotation marks with a citation and page number. Sometimes italics are used to distinguish such quotes from the student's work. Longer quotes are usually given a separate paragraph and indented. What have I said about longer quotes?'

'You told me not to use quotes unless the form of words is critical, so I suppose that long quotes aren't popular.'

'Not popular at all! Sometimes we get work that consists of a string of quotes. You can imagine that this doesn't score too highly. Or quotes suspended between two paragraphs with no indication of which paragraph the quote refers to. A colleague of mine calls these "hanging quotes" and he hates them.'

'I suppose any assignment that's just a string of quotes lacks criticality.'

'Absolutely! Now while we're talking about the layout of your work, let's end this session by considering tables and figures. What's the difference?'

'A table is a table and a figure is a figure,' I responded, sounding like a character out of *Alice in Wonderland*.

'A table is a table, but what's a figure?'

'Now you've got me!'

'Anything that's not a table.' Now Richard sounded like a character out of Alice.

'You mean graphs, diagrams, pictures and charts?' I asked.

'Exactly! Again, this may sound pernickety, but it's important that your work communicates your meaning effectively. Remember that half the battle of academic writing is getting your message across – communicating and explaining complex ideas clearly and concisely – and there are conventions for this. So a table is a table and it is labelled in the text as "Table 1" etcetera. You may also see "Table 2.1". This convention is used in longer accounts and it means that the table in question is Table 1 in Chapter 2. This helps the reader to find the table without looking through the whole account. This convention is applied to figures too. Don't forget to add a legend to tables and figures.'

'You mean a title?'

'No, a title usually goes at the top of a figure and is very brief. A legend goes underneath and it says just a little more than a title.'

Sam's reflection

16 October

Much as I find referencing a pain in the neck it's pretty clear that it's important. Especially with all the attention that lecturers are giving to plagiarism. I suppose I'll have to try once and for all to crack the problem. I imagine that once you have learnt how to reference properly it becomes second nature and you don't even have to think about it. Anyway, I hereby resolve to read and learn the Harvard System. Then I can become one of those people who are always harping on about poor referencing and how it is indicative of a drop in academic standards.

Record of tutorial

Student: Sam Sylon　　　　　　　　　　　　**Date: 11/10/XX**

SUMMARY OF KEY LEARNING POINTS

It is essential that you:

- Identify a clear conceptual framework as early as possible as this will help you focus your reading.
- Find a seminal source that 'opens the door' to the literature.
- Identify key words and phrases that you can use in your searches.
- Start your literature search with a visit to the library. Spend some time just reviewing what journals and books are available in your area of interest. Explore what electronic resources and searches are available and remember to act with 'purpose'.
- Start writing your literature review immediately. As your research progresses this will inform and be informed by your findings.
- Identify the key themes in your work and organise a filing system for recording relevant material. As an aid to identification use colour coding.
- Be critical. Don't just accept what the writer says, ask yourself why s/he has said it. Is it based on evidence or is it just their bias or ideology talking?
- Follow referencing conventions.
- Avoid plagiarism at all costs.
- Use quotes sparingly.
- Consider using bibliographic packages. For small-scale research projects they are unnecessary. A manual system or a simple database will do. However, knowing how to use them is a useful transferable skill.
- Number and label figures and tables correctly.
- Check the university guides for guidelines on presentation of work.
- Have a look at **http://scholar.google.co.uk/**.

➡

Agreed action points

Sam will:

- Obtain a copy of the library's guide to referencing and learn how to apply the Harvard Referencing System.

- Manually review the education journals held by the library and identify those which are relevant to the research.

- Undertake a range of electronic searches using the British Education Index and Google Scholar and refine searches using a variety of key words.

The literature review

Use the focal paragraph and research questions to identify precisely which aspects of the subject you need to review

⬇

List key concepts, theories or words for use in your search

⬇

Literature search

- Books
- Non-government reports
- Government reports
- Peer reviewed journals
- TES/THES/Economist/etc
- Professional publications e.g. unions
- Teachers' TV/radio and TV sources
- Broadsheet newspapers
- College/school/university VLE
- Internet

⬇

Separate the interesting from the essential. Summarise the essential and contrast views/theories expressed

⬇

Write the draft literature review → Use to explain, analyse and evaluate your data

⬇

Remove literature not used to analyse/contextualise your data. Add new literature required to critique findings ⬅

⬇

Amend, edit and polish the final literature review

Handout

SOURCES OF LITERATURE IN ORDER OF ACADEMIC CREDIBILITY

- Peer reviewed journals with an international reputation.
- Peer reviewed journals with a national reputation.
- Seminal books by authors with a high academic reputation.
- Books by authors with a high academic reputation.
- Act of Parliament, White Papers, Green Papers, Government reports, Reports and papers from local government and quasi-autonomous governmental organisations (QUANGOS), e.g. OfSTED. Note that these reports, while important, are not unbiased.
- Professional journals including publications by professional bodies, trade unions and employer organisations.
- Quality press publications such as *The Times Educational Supplement, The Times Higher Education, The Economist, The Spectator.*
- The broadsheet newspapers, including *The Times, Guardian, Independent* and *Telegraph.*
- TV and Radio quality documentaries and Teachers TV.
- You will note that no mention has been made of the Internet. This is because websites range in academic quality from the highly respectable and influential to absolute dross. When using websites it is imperative that you critically evaluate the provenance of the site. For example who funds and runs the site, what is its editorial policy and how often is the material on it updated?

Additional information on the issues covered by this tutorial can be found at/in:

- www.pearsoned.co.uk/colesmcgrath
- **Denscombe, M.** (2008) *The Good Research Guide (3rd ed.) McGraw Hill*: Maidenhead, Ch. 12 (Note this chapter looks at documents as data rather than literature, see Tutorial 7, but it is still useful)
- **Newby, P.** (2010) *Research Methods for Education*. Longman, Pearson: Harlow, Ch. 5

CHOOSING YOUR RESEARCH METHODOLOGY

Aim of tutorial

To assist you to decide which research methodology, quantitative or qualitative, is most suitable for your research. To achieve this both methodologies are defined and evaluated. Additionally, other aspects of methodology such as ethics, triangulation, validity and reliability are explored.

Contents

→ Qualitative versus quantitative methodologies

→ Generalisability

→ Ethics

→ Validity

→ Reliability

→ Sampling

→ Triangulation

→ Bias

Sam's reflection

25 October

Richard said that we were going to talk about research methodology today and review what is meant by the terms generalisability, ethics, validity, reliability, sampling, triangulation and bias. It all sounds very technical to me and I'm not sure that I see the point of it. I mean I can see why I need to be able to design and use questionnaires and interview schedules but what's the point of delving into the detail of the research process? I really don't want to go to tonight's session. Between this course and problems at work I'm shattered. But I suppose I must.

Review of tutorial

'Hi Sam.'

'Hello,' I said, feeling jaded and tired.

'That's rather half-hearted, I thought that you'd be up for this one.'

'Well, we have an inspection at work and the dog didn't look too well this morning, so I . . .'

'Thought wouldn't it be nice to have the night off.'

'I admit that I did think about cancelling the session.'

'I'm glad that you didn't. Choosing the correct research methodology is very important part of the research process. Anyway, I told my wife that I would be late for our salsa lesson tonight because I was seeing you. You can't imagine the grief I got. So it's a good job you're here.'

I hadn't really thought about the impact that cancelling at short notice might have on Richard and I felt glad that I had made the effort to attend.

'Anyway', he said, 'what we are going to look at today is quantitative and qualitative approaches to research. These two methodologies are often represented as opposing paradigms. With qualitative research exploring people's attitudes, beliefs, feelings and perceptions and quantitative research concerned with numbers, quantities and observable facts. But this oppositional view isn't very helpful. Most research contains elements of both approaches.'

'So what are the differences between the two approaches?'

'There are several and the easiest way for me to explain them is to pose them as a series of opposites. Very often the purpose of quantitative research is to test a theory or verify a claim. This may involve carrying out controlled experiments, counting or measuring some phenomena such as exam results. Data may be collected from statistical records, detailed observations, questionnaires or experiments. The idea is to be as objective as possible. To achieve this, the researcher tries to minimise any effect that their own beliefs, values and opinions might have on the data. They remain detached from the research participants and the data they collect from them. The nature of the data they're interested in is hard, impersonal and factual and they seek to generalise their findings across time and beyond the location in which they collect the data.'

Ask a silly question and get a complex answer I thought. There was a lot to take in but I decided to stay quiet and hear what he had to say about qualitative data.

'The purpose of qualitative research is to generate theories not to verify them. It is concerned with discovery rather than proof and the researcher attempts to collect data without interfering with the normal flow of life. Data can be collected using observations, interviews, questionnaires and focus groups and will describe attitudes, beliefs and feelings. However, the nature of the data means it isn't possible to accurately measure the phenomena under review. The values of the researcher and the relationship they have with the respondents also affect how the data are interpreted. Effectively the researcher uses their own knowledge, experience and understanding to make sense of it. The nature of the data that qualitative researchers are interested in will be complex, impressionistic, personal, soft and rich and it's impossible to communicate this adequately using numbers. The findings won't be generalisable but they will be relatable to similar situations and of interest to people in what appear quite different settings.'

'Why would people in different settings be interested?'

'Qualitative research is concerned with people and while the setting may change human nature stays the same. If you doubt me read "Meditations" by the Roman Emperor Marcus Aurelius.'

'Marcus Aurelius? Wasn't he in *Gladiator*?' I said, waiting for Richard to take the bait. Instead he just gave me a pitying look, his eyes turned towards heaven. I moved on quickly, 'From what you say it sounds as if my research is going to be qualitative.'

'I think it is fair to say that your work is broadly qualitative but it would be possible to fine-tune it and include an element of quantitative research.'

'OK,' I said doubtfully.

Richard smiled and continued. 'Don't look so worried. I'm sure you can cope with a few numbers.'

'But I don't have any numbers to analyse. I'm dealing solely with words. Why go out of my way to manufacture quantitative data?'

'There are several dimensions to doing a project like this. One of which is developing your skills as a researcher. My old Dad used to say "if the only tool you have in your bag is a hammer than every problem you see will look like a nail". We aim to provide you with a full toolkit. Only when you know the value of quantitative data and how to collect, analyse and use it will you be in a position to say with confidence that you don't require it.'

'OK,' I said, 'but I still can't see what useful quantitative data I could collect.'

'You intend to use questionnaires with the children. What sort of questions do you intend to ask?'

'I was going to use some Likert style questions and ask them to say on a scale of one to five how they felt about a series of questions.' As I spoke I realised that I would have plenty of numbers to report. 'OK,' I said sheepishly, 'I've got numbers.'

Richard grinned. 'You have indeed. However, you should realise that what you would be doing is reporting qualitative data in a quantitative form because the rating given by the children is effectively just a descriptor of their qualitative feelings and perceptions. In addition, whenever you assess people's opinions there will always be variation in how they interpret and understand the question you've asked. This is why caution is needed when analysing semi-quantitative data such as this. It can be like "castles built on sand"; there is the danger that you will make quantitative claims without adequate foundation.'

Sam's reflection

26 October

This was an eye-opener. I'd heard of quantitative and qualitative methodologies previously, but I thought that they were two completely separate approaches. Now I realise that my project is like a recipe. I can add in a taste of the quantitative if I want to.

It's probably too simplistic to say that qualitative research deals in words and quantitative research in numbers but I find that a simple way to describe the difference between them.

I wonder if my aversion to quantitative research is based on my fear of maths. I'm certainly more confident dealing with words but I shouldn't be worried about analysing numbers. After all, they're just statistics and that's only one step up from arithmetic. Is that me just whistling in the dark? No, be positive, there is a tutorial on analysing quantitative data and there is no reason why I can't master it. On that positive note I'm going to watch 'West Wing' and go to bed.

Review of tutorial

'Now linked to the choice of methodology are questions about generalisability, ethics, validity, reliability, triangulation and bias. Do you remember that we briefly mentioned them in Tutorial 2?'

'Yes,' I said uncertainly.

'Well you need to write a paragraph or so on each of them in your Methodology chapter, so let's start with generalisability. As I just said, generalisability relates to how far your findings are applicable across the board. For example, if you were researching the behaviour of year three children in an inner city school in Birmingham could you claim that your findings are applicable to all year three classes in England?'

'No,' I said firmly. 'The issues facing an inner city school in Birmingham are very different from those in a leafy suburb in Kent.'

'Exactly, they're not comparable. How might you make them more comparable?'

I had to think about that but finally said, 'You could include different schools from different areas of the country.'

'You could. What you're suggesting is that you need a more representative sample. But is that practical given that you are a sole researcher with a deadline fast approaching?'

'No.'

'Correct. In general, qualitative findings tend to be unique to a particular time and place and to the people that took part in the research. Whereas the results from large-scale quantitative projects are very often generalisable because the sample selected is statistically representative of whatever group or population you are looking at. However, this is unlikely to be the case in a small-scale quantitative project. So don't claim that your work is generalisable. Instead suggest that it is relatable.'

Sam's reflection

27 October

I had assumed that to be any good my research would have to apply to all schools or at least a good number of them. It's a comfort to realise that it doesn't have to. I suppose this goes back to something Richard said at our first meeting: research at this level is about improving professional knowledge and/or practice. It is not about solving the problems of the world. So all I'm going to claim for my research is that it's relatable to schools similar to mine and that aspects of the research might be of interest to other schools. Maybe that's one reason to make sure that I disseminate my findings within the school as they may well be particularly important to other staff as they relate to their circumstances.

Review of tutorial

'So what about ethical considerations?' I asked.

'A good place to start is the British Educational Research Association website **www.bera.ac.uk**. They publish a set of ethical guidelines that education researchers should follow. The main ones that you need to consider are: do no harm, obtain informed consent from all participants, respect participants' anonymity and abide by all legal requirements, including those of child protection and data protection. Now let's take each one of these in turn.'

I settled back in my chair and waited.

'You should never undertake research that can harm the participants physically, mentally or emotionally. That's why your project has to be approved before you can start to collect data. Unfortunately, it is not always possible to predict if a particular piece of research will upset or harm participants, so you need to be constantly on the lookout for any signs of distress and if you notice any you must suspend your research.'

'I know that causing no harm is important when dealing with children. But what do I need to look out for in particular?'

'When dealing with children or vulnerable adults you need to be very careful as there are specific legal obligations. Under these circumstances, guardians or other responsible adults – in this case "responsible" is used in a legal sense and could mean social workers – need to be involved to ensure that no harm results from any research undertaken and that only **authentic data** are collected.'

'This sounds like a right minefield. How does any research get done in schools?'

'The general position is that permission from parents or guardians isn't necessary if the research is part of the researcher's normal professional role. So gathering assessment data, pupils' work or the evaluation of lessons is usually acceptable. But it is vital to check with the head that these general permissions apply in your school. Parental permission is vital when photographs or video recordings are used. Some schools have a standard letter signed by parents for this, but you must check. You also need to ensure that you comply with the legal requirements for working with children and vulnerable adults; this usually means having the appropriate enhanced CRB check, which I assume you have.'

'Yes,' I said.

'Linked to the above concept is obtaining informed consent. This is difficult for teachers when they are researching their own pupils. For example, if you give your class a questionnaire to complete they're likely to believe that they must complete it. How much free choice is there in that? You must explain to all your participants the nature and purpose of your research and emphasise that they are under no obligation to take part in the research and that they can withdraw from it at any stage.'

'That could cause a problem if at a later stage a group of children say they want to withdraw because I cancelled their visit to the theatre.'

'That's true, but you must give them that option and honour your commitment to them. This is why it's useful to think of sources of data from your everyday practice, such as children's work and assessment results. These are 'authentic' too and less subject to bias.'

'What about confidentiality and anonymity?'

'Anonymity is certainly important. You must make it clear to participants that their identity will not be revealed . . .'

'Because they may not be as frank and honest with me if they think that they might be identified.'

'Precisely. What people say to you may harm them if their identity is revealed. For example if a teacher criticises the head or board of governors. So use pseudonyms such as "Teacher A" or "Pupil Alpha". If you use common names such as Bill or Mary as a pseudonym mention this in order to avoid any confusion. But even where you have used a pseudonym it's important that you don't reveal the person's identity by providing other information which enables the reader to identify the person. So if the school has four maths teachers, three of whom are in their twenties, it will be obvious who you speaking of if you say, "One maths teacher who has worked at the school for over 20 years said . . ."'

'What about data protection?' I asked.

Richard took a deep breath and said, 'That's a good example of a legal and an ethical requirement. You should only hold data necessary for the research and it must be disposed of in a secure way as soon as possible. Unlike the British Secret Service be particularly careful with data on laptops and memory sticks and ensure that paper is securely shredded.'

Sam's reflection

27 October

I thought that the ethical side was really going to be a tick-box exercise. A case of 'going through the motions'. But I realise now that it's much more important than that. I have important responsibilities to the people taking part in my research and it's vital that they don't suffer in any way as a result. In addition, if things do go wrong I need to demonstrate that I acted responsibly at every stage of the process.

The 'normal professional role' bit was interesting. This seems to mean that I can carry out research in school if it is connected to my normal duties. I still need the Head's approval. But that's no bad thing as it's important to get management's support for what I am doing and any changes that I might want to recommend.

It's occurred to me that Richard used the word 'authentic' data'. He used it in passing, but knowing him there's more to it than I think. 'Authentic' means 'real', 'genuine' or 'valid', which is what you want your data to be. After all, what's the point if my data doesn't bear some relation to the real situation?

Review of tutorial

'Now we need to discuss "validity". What do you think "validity" means?'

'Well a valid opinion is one that is based on a good argument or evidence,' I ventured. 'So I assume that valid research is research which is based on firm foundations.'

'Very good. We just need to tweak it very slightly because some terms have a slightly different meaning to the normal when used in a technical sense. In this case we're really talking about the validity of your approach. A "valid" approach is one that ensures that you actually measure what you intended to measure. This is why we make such a fuss about the research questions. When you say that you're measuring such things as "enjoyment", "motivation", or "engagement", you need to ensure that you use an approach that will actually measure these things. So, how would you measure "enjoyment"?'

'I'd ask the participants if they enjoyed the activity.'

'What does "enjoy" mean?'

'Now you're pulling my leg. I know what "enjoy" means and so do they.'

'But do they? This word means different things to different people; its interpretation is subjective. One person's enjoyment is another's greatest moment in their life. So you need to define "enjoyment" and be clear that the questions you ask relate to your definition.'

'Because then I would be measuring what I set out to measure.'

'Exactly! Of course some aspects of your approach will be more valid than others and the task here is to comment on which aspects are more or less valid and what could be done to improve validity. The important thing is that you demonstrate your understanding of the concept and explain how you dealt with it. So often people write "my approach was valid because . . ." There are always aspects that are more valid than others.'

Without pause Richard continued, 'Once you've covered validity you can look at its partner, reliability. Reliability is concerned with the question, "to what extent would I get the same results if I were to repeat the research again?"'

'I can see a problem with that right away. With a scientific experiment it's possible to get the same result time after time. But I can't interview the same person twice and expect exactly the same answers.'

'Good! That's another difference between quantitative and qualitative research. Very often in quantitative research you can repeat the research and get very similar results whereas this is not possible in qualitative research.'

'So how do you ensure reliability in qualitative research?'

'It's a matter of transparency. You need to describe how you carried out your research in sufficient detail to enable others to repeat your work if they wish to. You provide what is known as an "**audit trail**". For example you will need to explain how you drew up and tested your questionnaire, how you selected and approached your respondents and exactly how the questionnaire was administered and analysed.'

28 October

Previously I wasn't too keen about revealing any weaknesses in my research. But I can now see why it is important to critically evaluate my approach. Only if I'm critical can I identify and address issues surrounding validity and reliability. So I need to identify those aspects of my work that help validity and reliability and those that have detracted from it and suggest ways that I might improve them in the future.

Review of tutorial

Something had been bubbling away at the back of my mind and I finally I asked, 'Would the sample you selected affect validity and reliability?'

'Yes, a random sample that was large enough to be statistically significant would help reliability. But the samples in most small-scale research projects are neither genuinely random nor sufficiently large to be statistically significant.'

'So what are the main types of sample that students use?'

'A few try to use a random sample. They give each person in the **population** that they want to sample a number and then select numbers at random. The problem is that humans are always looking for patterns so we are very poor at picking numbers at random.'

'What about putting the numbers in a hat?'

'Better, but not perfect. What they need to use is a random number generator – Excel has one.'

'That sounds complex. Why can't you just grab the people who are in the staff room and use them,' I said, expecting him to explode with indignation.

'What you're talking about is convenience sampling and it does have its place, but I wouldn't recommend that you use it because it's hard to justify and makes you look lazy and slapdash.'

'But sometimes the people in the staffroom are the very ones you want to speak to because they have specific information that you require,' I said, still trying to avoid using random sampling.

'Now you are talking about purpositive sampling. This is where you choose certain people because they have the information you require.'

'I can do that can I?' I said, with surprise and relief.

'Indeed you can. In fact it is probably the most used sampling technique for small-scale qualitative research.'

'Great. It sounds a lot better than convenience sampling.'

'Clearly you understand the value of "spin" in what you write. You'll make a Head one day,' Richard said laughing. 'But it is also worth mentioning "stratified sampling". Any idea what that means?'

'Stratified means layered, so it probably means that I choose samples from different layers of the population.'

'In a sense yes. Essentially you select sub-populations relevant to your study and take samples from those.'

'OK, so I could split the population into males and females and take a sample from each group or split the children by year group?'

'Exactly.'

Sam's reflection

29 October

So sampling can be random, convenience, purposive or stratified. But it must also be possible to combine two or more methods. For example, I could have three separate groups, say senior managers, heads of year and teachers, and then use purposive sampling to select who I spoke to in each group. That's worth thinking about. I do like the idea of purposive sampling.

That said, Richard's Dad and his hammer is haunting me. I need to understand and explain each sampling technique and comment on how each might affect my results. Because only then will I be able to argue convincingly for the approach that I use.

Review of tutorial

'We've covered a lot today, but before we end there are a couple more things that need to be included in the methodology section. These are triangulation and bias.'

'Ah, I know about triangulation; it means that I should use three different research methods.'

'You're almost correct. What you're trying to do is view the issue that you're researching from more than one viewpoint. Why do you think this is important?'

'Is it about trying to see things from different angles?' I suggested.

'Exactly. If you look at an object from just one angle you only see one aspect or surface of it. If you look at it from a different angle previously unseen features may come into focus.'

'So how can I achieve this rounded view?'

'Well there are different types of triangulation. The ones which you might use include methodological triangulation. This involves the use of different methodologies such as quantitative and qualitative to get a fix on the situation. Using a mixed methodology approach you could compare and contrast what a teacher says in an interview (qualitative data) about improving performance with the schools SATS results from the last five years (quantitative data). In this way you're collecting data from two sources, each of which is underpinned by a different research methodology.'

'Would it matter if both methods were qualitative?'

'No it wouldn't, but then you would be using methods triangulation not methodological triangulation. For example, you might interview a group of teachers about the teaching methods that they use and compare this with your findings from a classroom observation. One method reveals what the teachers said they do and the second what they actually do. The two may well be the same but you would be surprised how often they differ.'

'I like the idea of methods triangulation. It sounds straightforward and doable,' I said.

'Many would agree with you. It's the most popular type of triangulation with students,' he said. 'But you might also want to consider data source triangulation. This is where you collect data on the same topic from different groups of participants. For example, in your assignment you could collect data from parents, teachers and children. This would give you a more rounded picture of the issue.'

'I'm looking at children in different year groups. Does that count?' I interjected.

'That's a good point and yes it does count. So you need to say that in your write-up. The fourth type of triangulation involves collecting data at different times or more than once from your participants. This allows you to pick up on any changes in what people have to say as a result of the passage of time and the development of their ideas. Fifthly, and much more unlikely, you can use more than one researcher to collect the data. But by its vey nature it's not an approach that sole researchers can use.'

'Do I have to use each type of triangulation or can I rely on just one?'

'For most small-scale research projects you'll use only one or two approaches. The most common are methods triangulation and data source triangulation. If you use either of these approaches you gain a more complete picture of the issue that you are investigating and you improve the accuracy of the data you collect. This improved accuracy also helps you to claim validity for your work as you are measuring what you set out to measure from more than one standpoint.'

Sam's reflection

30 October

Triangulation is obviously important but I don't think that it is difficult to achieve. My research involves collecting data from pupils in different year groups so I will be able to claim data source triangulation.

Unfortunately even if I interview some teachers I won't be able to claim methods triangulation because the information they provide does not come from the same source as the data from the questionnaires, i.e. the children. To claim methods triangulation I would have to interview some of the children.

Review of tutorial

'So that just leaves bias. I don't think that it will be much of a problem as I don't think that any of my participants have any extreme views.'

'If only it were that easy. Bias is always present and it doesn't necessarily come from people with extreme views. The nature of qualitative research is that people's opinions are based on their whole life experience and will be affected by more than the issue under consideration. Even with quantitative research bias is possible because particular samples are chosen or the data may be analysed in a way which favours a particular result.'

'I thought that bias was something that my participants would show, I didn't realise that I could be the source.'

'The researcher always influences the result . . .'

'And my task is to evaluate the possible effect on my findings.'

'Correct. In the case of research when do you think that your bias surfaces for the first time?'

'When you start to write up your findings?' I suggested.

'I think it starts with your choice of topic.'

'If that's the case then you can never produce a piece of unbiased research. That can't be right.'

'In the case of scientific research where you're dealing with inanimate objects it is easier to reduce bias to negligible levels. The researcher doesn't have an emotional or social relationship with the "participants" involved. But in the social sciences research bias starts with your choice of topics. What you choose to research says something about your own interests and what you think is important. Therefore it's virtually impossible for the social science researcher to come to a topic without some prior knowledge or opinion about the issues involved. In all probability it's that prior knowledge which has attracted them to the topic. Effectively, it is not possible for the researcher to come to the research with "an empty mind". The best they can hope for is an "open mind".'

This sounded like one of those problems that had no real solution. But I tried anyway and asked, 'So how do I deal with bias in my research?'

'Firstly you need to recognise that whatever you write will contain an element of bias. Secondly, you need to demonstrate that you've attempted to counter your own bias by using a good range of writers in your literature review, some of whom you agree with and others you don't. Thirdly, when analysing the data look for alternative interpretations, especially if the findings confirm your own views. Try to challenge your own interpretations. Fourthly, explain to the reader how you carried out your research, analysed your data and your thinking behind the key decisions that you made. This will enable them to judge for themselves to what extent your findings and interpretations are a reasonable representation of the situation.'

'It also helps me to claim reliability,' I interjected. 'It's all about telling the reader what you've done, how you did it and why you did it. It's about leaving an audit trail.'

'Exactly. That is a really good way to think about it. But it is also important to consider to what extent you are an "insider" or an "outsider".'

'I remember this. I'm an insider because I'm working with colleagues and my own pupils. That will affect how they see and respond to me. They may give me the answer that they think I want to hear.'

'True, but of course if you were an outsider – possibly a researcher working for the local authority – the same problem may arise. This is really about the role of the researcher. It's difficult but you do need to consider how your relationship with others in your study could influence the result. Talking about relationships with others, I need to get to that salsa lesson or I'll be the outsider tonight and I'll be sleeping in the shed! I suggest that you have a look at the handout on the advantages and disadvantages of **insider research** and we can discuss it at our next session if you have any queries. For now let's agree your action points.'

Sam's reflection

31 October

Welcome to the world of paranoia. From what Richard says it seems that everything I say, write and think is drenched in bias. How am I supposed to get around that? I suppose what I need to do is to think carefully about what I write and try and understand why I've interpreted the data the way I have. Sometimes what I think will be entirely reasonable – such as hating marking. That's just normal, a part of every teacher's DNA. Isn't it?

But I do need to challenge my views and opinions, test them against the evidence and see what other points of view are valid. Then I need to make sure that they are fairly represented in my work. Hang on – a ping moment has just occurred – if I end up with an interpretation of the data that is unexpected or which I don't like that is probably a good sign, or is it?

Record of tutorial

Student: Sam Sylon   **Date: 25/10/XX**
SUMMARY OF KEY LEARNING POINTS

- Qualitative approaches are about subjective attitudes and beliefs. The unit of analysis is words and while the responses are unique to the location in which they were collected, the findings may be relatable to similar situations.

- Quantitative approaches are objective and are often about measurement of phenomena. The unit of analysis is numbers. Findings may be generalisable depending on how representative the sample was.

- Quantitative and qualitative approaches can be combined.

- Care needs to be taken when making quantitative judgements from qualitative data.

- Key ethical issues are: do no harm, protect the participants' well-being and maintain their anonymity. This is particularly important when dealing with children and vulnerable adults. Obtain genuine informed consent from all participants and ensure that they understand their right to withdraw at any stage. Obtain permission from all stakeholders prior to starting the research and observe all data protection requirements.

- Validity is concerned with ensuring that the data collection methods used actually measure or describe the phenomena the researcher is interested in.

- In quantitative research reliability relates to what extent the data collection methods used would give the same or similar results if repeated. In qualitative research reliability is concerned with the reasonableness of the approach adopted and the decisions made by the researcher.

- Sampling may be random, purposive, convenience, stratified, or a combination of these.

- Triangulation means looking at the data from more than one angle. There are different types of triangulation including: methodological, methods, data source, time delay and multiple researcher.

- Bias is always present because people are involved in research. Bias can result from participants or researchers.

Agreed action points

Sam will:

- Review the final list of research questions and determine which research methodology is most suitable to use and why.
- Obtain and read a copy of the BERA ethical guidelines from www.bera.ac.uk.
- Identify which sampling method to use.
- Consider how to deal with validity, reliability, triangulation and bias when designing the research programme.

Approaches to research – qualitative and quantitative methodologies

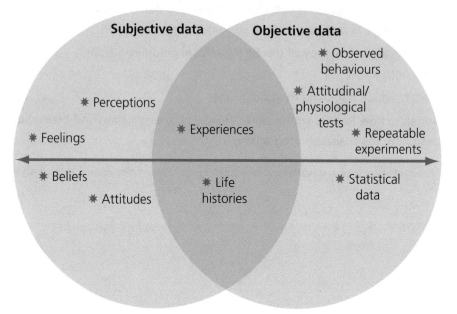

Note: the placement of the ✳ indicates where on the subjective/objective continuum each descriptor resides.

Handout

RESEARCHING IN FAMILIAR SETTINGS – STRENGTHS AND WEAKNESSES

Strengths	Weaknesses
Familiarity with the setting may mean that the researcher isn't surprised by what they see.	Familiarity with the setting means that the researcher may not challenge his/her own assumptions about the organisation.
The researcher blends into the background and is accepted by the respondents, so suspicion may be less.	The researcher's new role may be challenged by participants.
The researcher may have a good relationship with participants.	The power and professional relationships between the researcher and the respondent may become unclear during the process.
The researcher's prior knowledge can help identify the most pertinent issues in the organisation.	Knowledge of the setting can lead to the researcher ignoring everyday events and practices.
It's easier for the researcher to access people and places.	The organisation's management may influence the researcher implicitly or explicitly.
The researcher may be more trusted by the participants.	The researcher may be judged by staff as a result of prior knowledge and there may be an impact on future relationships.
The researcher is in a better position to judge whether participants are likely to respond accurately.	The researcher may think that the participants share his/her views and this may bias the analysis of findings.
Researcher possesses a great deal of insider knowledge that can assist the research.	The researcher may not be aware of or may be misguided about relevant issues in the organisation.
	Anonymity may be a significant ethical issue as the researcher may be known by the participants.
	The participants may not take the researcher/research seriously and instead engage in 'game playing'.

(After Hockey 1993; Robson 1993).

Additional information on the issues covered by this tutorial can be found at/in:

- www.pearsoned.co.uk/colesmcgrath
- Cohen, L., Mannion, L. and Morrison, K. (2007) *Research Methods in Education (6th ed.).* Routledge Falmer: London, Ch. 1.
- Newby, P. (2010) *Research Methods for Education.* Longman, Pearson: Harlow, Chs. 2, 3.

RESEARCH STRATEGIES – CASE STUDIES, ACTION RESEARCH AND SURVEYS

Aim of tutorial

To enable you to select the most appropriate strategy for your research from case study, action research or survey. To achieve this each strategy is defined and evaluated.

Contents

→ Choosing the right research strategy

→ The range of approaches

→ Case studies

→ Action research

→ Surveys

Sam's reflection

5 November

Today we're looking at research strategies. I'm not entirely sure how these fit into the scheme of things. We've already discussed methodology which covered quantitative versus qualitative approaches and issues such as validity and reliability. And I know that in the future we'll be looking at data collection methods so I wonder how research strategies differ from these?

Richard said that we would discuss case studies, action research and surveys. So what do I know about these terms? I've come across the word 'case' as in a legal case or a social worker's case. Both of these 'cases' focus on a single person and from working with social workers I know that these files are very detailed. So for a case study I would probably have to say who was involved, what they did and what were the sources of evidence that I used.

Action research sounds as if some action is taken and the researcher then describes what took place. But who does the action, the researcher or the people involved in the research? I think it's probably the researcher.

Surveys seem simpler. These would be about canvassing people's opinion. And most surveys only collect data from a sample of people don't they? I'm not sure if this is always the case, I'd better check. I wonder if these are the only strategies that researchers can use? I finish work early today. I'll pop into the library before tonight's session and see what other strategies are available.

Review of tutorial

I arrived early, excited by what I'd found in the library. Richard waved me into a chair.

'How are things?' he asked.

'Fine,' I said, 'I've got loads of questions.'

'That's good. It's always valuable when people prepare for the tutorial in advance. That way they can set the agenda and drive the discussion in the direction that meets their needs. So fire away.'

'You said that we would discuss three research strategies today. Case studies, action research and surveys. But I've been looking in the library and different authors refer to these as methodologies or methods and I've not found any that describe them as strategies, so I'm confused?'

'Welcome to the debate on research. One of the odd things about research is that for a process which demands precision and detail there is precious little agreement on the definitions for many of the terms commonly used. Some writers talk about case studies as a research method and describe qualitative or quantitative research as an approach to research rather than a methodology. What I try to do in these tutorials is simplify the discussion and just have three levels which students can easily understand. At the top level you have the broad philosophical and conceptual issues such as what is the nature of the research, quantitative or qualitative, and how do I know that what I am reporting has validity and is reliable. I call this the research methodology. Basically the methodology is concerned with the overarching principles and the structure of the research. But that's pretty vague. It needs shaping. To do this I use the term research strategies, such as the case study, action research and survey that we'll discuss today. These strategies help me to organise and structure the research; to delineate the boundaries of the research and maintain control over the project. And finally I have research methods which are the tools I use to collect the data such as interviews and questionnaires. My approach is basically a three-stage process that moves from the abstract to the strategic and then to the practical.'

'OK,' I said a little uncertainly, still unsure that I fully understood. Undaunted I asked, 'But aren't there more strategies than just the three you've listed. I've just been reading about ethnography for example?'

'Good question. There's a whole range of different strategies available and it's important to choose the most appropriate one for your research. It's almost certain that you could justify using several different ones. But the vast majority of small-scale educational research projects or dissertations such as yours are covered by case studies, action research and surveys. These are conceptually straightforward, easy to grasp and flexible enough to address a range of research questions. It's also the case that action research has become the method of choice to support professional development in professions such as teaching, nursing and social work. As for ethnography, certainly it is not an approach that I would suggest for undergraduates or for very many Master level students.'

'So we won't be talking about ethnographies?'

'We can come back to them later.'

Sam's reflection

6 November

OK I need to get this clear in my head. There are three levels to the research process, viz:

- Methodology
- Strategy
- Methods.

I suppose I could liken it to management in my school. The board of governors and head set out the vision, the overall approach. That's the methodology. The senior management team work out the best way to deliver the vision. That's the strategy. And teachers select the right tools to get the job done. That's the methods. It's not a perfect analogy but it will do for now.

Review of tutorial

'So what is a case study?' asked Richard.

'I've been thinking about this. I think it's a detailed study of a person or event.'

'Not bad. They may certainly be about people and events but they can also be about phenomena, dyslexia for example.'

'Or a particular change to the National Curriculum.'

'Indeed. Essentially, a case study is the exploration of a bounded **instance** using multiple data collection methods which results in a highly detailed picture of the person, place or thing under examination. And it may involve some element of observation.'

'What do you mean by bounded?'

'Well it would be possible to look at the reaction of one person to an issue, a small group, a large group or the entire population of the country. As a researcher you have to find some way to limit the size of your enquiry . . .'

'Because what I'm after is a detailed picture which I couldn't get if I tried to collect data from too many people.'

'Precisely. So what boundaries might you set for your research?'

'Boundaries? Do you mean limits?'

'Yes, though "boundary" is the correct term to use so you could just look at one person, one class, one year group or just boys. So are you doing a case study?'

'Maybe,' I said doubtfully.

'Be careful. Are you going to use multiple data collection methods?'

'Well I'm going to use questionnaires with the kids and I might interview some teachers. Would that count as multiple methods?'

'Your instance is children's perceptions of their own safety. Therefore you would use questionnaires and interview some of them to get the detail necessary to build a three dimensional picture of their perceptions. You still might do that. But if you do then, rather than look at all children between the age of 7 and 11, I would suggest that you only look at one year group.'

'Because otherwise I would be collecting too much data.'

'Exactly! You would need to bound your study to manageable proportions.'

'OK. So what exactly do you mean by instance?'

'It's as I said, the subject of a case study can be a person, a group of people, a process or an event. Indeed it can be just about any phenomenon that has a discernable identity which marks it out as separate.'

'We're back to a boundary again. Are there any criteria I can use to help me select and define an instance?'

'There are many, but some common ones are an instance which is particularly interesting or atypical, such as a group of pupils who don't speak English at home. Or a unique event such as an educational exchange between schools. And let's not forget that extreme instances can be interesting . . .'

'Like looking at the most or least able pupils in a class?'

'Yes, that's a particularly common choice. But so too is the situation where your boss asks you to look at a particular issue which you can then construct as a case study. Of course one problem with case studies is that it's very unlikely that you'll find examples of the same case study in the literature and because it is unique to your situation the findings won't be generalisable to other situations.'

'But it might be relatable?'

'True. What you want to do is to derive descriptions from the study that can be related to similar circumstances. How might "other circumstances" be similar?'

'They could have happened at the same time, in similar places or organisations or with a similar group of people.'

'Or under similar circumstances. Excellent. So going back to the example of a case study that looks at a school exchange, while you might be unable to find an evaluation of an exchange with say a school in Ljubljana, you would certainly find information on the impact of educational exchanges. Equally, other schools in the area may have had exchanges with other countries, so your experiences would still interest them. So, before we move on can you suggest some advantages and disadvantages of the case study strategy?'

'You always put me on the spot!' I said. 'Well I suppose advantages would be things like the use of different methods and sources of data as they would help triangulation and validity. I can also make the project doable by setting sensible boundaries and I would be looking at something distinct and original. It also seems like a natural approach as I'm not changing anything. I'm just looking at what's there.'

'And disadvantages?'

'You've said that I can't generalise, I can only relate. I'm struggling a bit. It seems a good strategy to me.'

'**True, though one of your advantages could also be a disadvantage. If you're setting the boundaries ...**'

'Then I could introduce bias. Although I'm not intervening I may still influence the outcome in some way, particularly if I know the people involved. And I may end up wasting precious time collecting too much data from my multiple data collection methods.'

Sam's reflection

10 November

If I reduced the number of children I collect data from then the case study strategy would be suitable for my project. It would give me the opportunity to use several different methods and get a much more detailed picture of what's going on. But against that my research will only represent the views of some of the children. What do I want: a small detailed picture or a large sketch of what is going on? I'm not sure. I really need to think about what I want to get out of the research and how useful it will be to the children and the school. Best to go back to my research questions I think.

Review of tutorial

'So what do you think action research is about then?'

'Action implies doing something. Evaluation is important in research, so something is done and it's then evaluated. I'm not sure who does it though. Me or someone else?'

'OK. Let's flesh that out a bit. There are a number of different interpretations of the action research strategy. The term was first used by Kurt Lewin. He was an American academic and the context was very much about exploring strategies for social change and the principle was one of planning and implementing a social change followed by evaluation. However, the "British tradition" is one of practice or practitioner-based research with the goal of self-improvement.'

'That seems a bit self-centred. Surely professionals would want to have a positive impact on others in some way?'

'The implication is that self-improvement would inevitably result in a positive impact on others, indeed the core of action research is that it's social and involves the community. Your use of the word "impact" is important though. One of the key criteria for using action research as a model for professional development is that it does have an impact, let's say on pupils' learning. Self-evaluation is critical though and the philosophy is that this should be ongoing and not just be done at the end of the project.'

'But how do you actually do it?' I asked, feeling that I still had no clear idea of what action research was.

'It's a cyclical process that starts with identifying a problem. Say you want to improve boys' achievement in reading. You benchmark the existing position by collecting assessment scores. You then collect data from the children and other teachers using interviews, observations or questionnaires to try to identify the problems. This is called "baseline data". You reflect on the data collected and design a series of changes or **interventions** in how boys are taught to read in your target group. You then implement a single change, monitor it and assess what impact it had. Only then do you implement another change. You keep going through this cycle until you are satisfied with the boys' level of achievement.'

'It sounds like a reflective diary would be very useful,' I said.

'Almost essential. What did you do? How did you do it? What effect did it have and how will you change the situation or process to make it better? I've seen some reflective diaries that have clearly been typed at the end of the project, they're almost useless. I've also seen fantastic examples where people have taken the "scrapbook" approach and included diagrams, mind maps. Examples of pupils work to illustrate points, news items. Great work.'

'I remember someone at work doing an action research project. They implemented a new maths package and evaluated it by collecting pupils' work. I don't recall what else they changed if anything and I don't think they kept a research diary. So was that action research? It sounds more like a case study to me!'

'I was hoping that you wouldn't ask that question! The accepted model is one where the practitioner implements an intervention, but subjects it to ongoing modification as a result of evaluating evidence. But remember that research methods are evolving; they're dynamic and people's understanding of them changes. A more recent version is that baseline evidence is gathered which describes the situation as it is. A single large-scale intervention is designed in the light of this evidence and implemented and the changes that result from this action are evaluated and reported. There is very little ongoing evaluation in this process and frankly the sponsors of this type of research aren't too bothered. What they want to see is an improvement in the situation.'

'I suppose that the impact is the most important thing, however it's been achieved,' I said.

'That's true, but the professional learning that takes place is also very important. Impact on one occasion may not continue unless there's some evidence that the practitioner has learnt something from the process and that this will influence their future behaviour.'

'I can see that this is a touchy subject.'

'Not really, but there are competing agendas. It's ok to adopt the new approach which is comprised of just a single intervention. That's fine. But, you need to explain why you have done this rather than use the traditional cyclical approach in your research methodology chapter.'

'OK, so how should I carry out an action research project?'

'Certainly plan to keep a research diary and expect to modify your approach as a result of your observations. Begin by collecting "baseline" data of the status quo.

Use the baseline data to justify your intervention. What is the target group, what are their needs as evidenced from diverse sources such as the levels of their work, colleagues' opinions, classroom observations by you and others? Remember the importance of authenticity in your data. Don't forget the conceptual framework and use evidence from diverse literature such as self-evaluation documents, OfSTED reports, subject association literature and Government reports to inform your planned intervention. Then design and implement your change.'

'And what if it doesn't work?' I asked.

'Be prepared to change or abandon your intervention. It's just the same as with your teaching. If you find that a particular teaching method or resource isn't working, you don't continue to use it regardless of outcomes. You change it in some way in order to meet your needs.'

'It strikes me that a research report based on action research could look quite different from some of the others. Where does all this information go?'

'Sometimes a portfolio approach is possible, though this can be very time-consuming and it isn't always good preparation for writing up more formal projects. The literature review still applies as a means to summarise your reading. The methodology is relevant as you need to explain your understanding of action research and how it was implemented, including the intervention. Of course aspects such as validity, reliability, triangulation and ethics will always apply. In fact there can be more ethical implications as you may well be very closely involved with the participants. The findings section may be slightly different in that you would present your baseline evidence, explain how this may have influenced your intervention and then present and evaluate the evidence of impact. This is where you could introduce evidence from your reflective diary if appropriate.'

'So it's a movable feast in many ways?'

'Not exactly, but try not to be too dogmatic. Explain and justify your strategy and be prepared to critique it in terms of other strategies such as case study and survey. The critical thing is that you justify the strategy you use in terms of the research objectives and, above all, try to be critical of accepted definitions and how your project relates to these. Also, try to ensure that you collect evidence of impact as this is the main purpose of action research and what managers and funding bodies want to see.'

'But how can I be sure that it was my intervention that caused the improvement observed and not something else?' I asked.

'You can't. Without a control group, this is very difficult to establish. However, you can compare achievement by current groups with that of similar groups before the intervention. If in the longer term raised achievement is sustained when the intervention continues, then you move closer to establishing that causal relationship.'

'It all sounds exciting and highly relevant to my practice, so I can appreciate its attractiveness. I think I could also sell it to my employer too, which is useful because they don't always see the relevance of my studies to work and are reluctant to pay my course fees. So what about the advantages and disadvantages of action research?'

'I was afraid you were going to ask. The advantages would include a close relevance to practice, stakeholders and the researcher. Diverse evidence can be included, so that helps validity and triangulation and the evidence is likely to be authentic in the sense that it often comes from pupils, say, and is unlikely to be subject to bias.'

'And the disadvantages?'

'I suppose that it seems like painting by numbers: it's difficult to know for certain if your intervention has caused any change identified. It may just be that you're working harder as the teacher. The approach seems to be evolving and is a bit controversial. There also seems to be a focus on data collection and evaluation, rather than data analysis.'

Sam's reflection

14 November

I'm excited by the idea of action research. For the first time I can see a strong relevance to my practice, my institution and to my own professional development. But I'm worried that it could be difficult to comply with the accepted action research approach. This could leave me

➡

open to criticism, but Richard has told me not to worry about that and to have the confidence to justify my approach and be prepared to critique it in the light of accepted models, so maybe the advantages outweigh the disadvantages. Unfortunately it is not an approach that I can use for this piece of research. I won't be implementing any change, just collecting and analysing what children think and feel. Mind you, the data collected might suggest possible interventions that I could make in the future. Now that's an idea.

Review of tutorial

'So that leaves us with ...?'

'Surveys,' I said.

'What's a survey then?'

'A survey involves collecting data from a large number of people which could be either the entire population or a sample of them at a single point in time.'

'That's pretty good. So what data collection tools could you use to sample the population?'

'I could use questionnaires, interviews or focus groups.'

'You can also undertake observations. We'll talk more about questionnaires, interviews and observations in a later tutorial, but what are your initial thoughts on these methods?'

'Questionnaires are useful for larger samples and can be structured for easy analysis and they're straightforward to administer.'

'What about bias?'

'It's probably minimised because the researcher has less influence on the participants.'

'And interviews?'

'Smaller samples. They are usually less structured than questionnaires but this can improve the depth of information obtained. But they are more difficult to analyse and more prone to bias as the researcher has more influence, assuming they do the interview!'

'Good point! What about focus groups?'

'I could access more people than I could with interviews but fewer than I could if I used questionnaires. The actual meetings could be highly structured, semi-structured or unstructured.'

'Any key advantages?' Richard asked.

'I think that the great strength is that people can bounce ideas off each other.'

'So focus groups can really add another dimension in that sense.'

'Yes, I see what you mean. People don't discuss issues in questionnaires or interviews.'

'Observations can be a powerful data collection tool in surveys. They can be structured or unstructured and potentially the sample can be quite large. However, bias could be an issue if the researcher knows the group that is being observed and just the presence of an observer can change how people act. But they do reveal what people do, which is a great strength.'

'So the data is authentic if it has been collected in a natural situation.'

'That all depends on the impact the observer has on the situation.'

'Observations must be good for triangulation as you get that "extra dimension" you mentioned as the participants interact?', I said.

'Yes, good point.'

'One thing though. Are case studies and surveys mutually exclusive? Could I have a survey as part of my case study?'

'You need to assess the opinions of the participants somehow, so yes you could. Remember that these are not entirely separate strategies, so give me a link between case studies and action research.'

'I suppose that it's possible to do a case study on a piece of action research after it's happened. The instance would be the teacher, the pupils, the topic and the intervention.'

'Excellent, so these aren't mutually exclusive and they can be combined in accordance with the demands of the research questions. So a survey could be used to gather baseline evidence for action research.'

Sam's reflection

18 November

I do feel more comfortable with surveys. But I need to step outside my comfort zone. Essentially what I'm looking at is a range of strategies that can be combined in different ways and the label is then applied to the final combination. The strategies certainly seem to overlap. Which is probably why Richard kept emphasising that the definitions of these strategies are often contested. I really need to focus on my research questions and maybe the wider context of my practice and the needs of my colleagues and institution to arrive at an appropriate strategy. Maybe even then it wouldn't be absolutely 'right' and I would only know that after the event. I suppose that's what learning to be a researcher is all about, though I feel that it would take a lifetime to become an expert. Just look at Richard, he's had long enough, yet he still has his doubts.

Review of tutorial

'You said you'd come back to ethnography and other possible strategies.'

'Oh yes, I nearly forgot! Ethnography could be viewed as another strategy. The word ethnography comes from the Greek *ethnos*, meaning people, and *graphein*, meaning to write. So what sort of research does it relate to?'

'A strategy involving writing about people,' I suggested.

'Essentially yes, though in a broader context "people" refers to specified groups of people and their behaviours. The groups could be defined according to some common criterion such as religion or culture. Fieldwork is usually involved in the sense that you would need to immerse yourself in those people in order to understand them. You may also have heard about **phenomenology**.'

'Wait a minute, that sounds like it's about studying phenomena such as events.'

'In a sense, but really it's the conscious experience of events from the perspective of the individual. So you're exploring people's experiences, understanding and reaction to particular events. In truth phenomenology is really a branch of philosophy. Many of its followers think that the whole of human knowledge can be explained in this way.'

'It sounds interesting. But I don't think it's particularly relevant for my project.'

'That's probably true, but **grounded theory** is another one worth a mention. This strategy is interesting as it is almost the reverse of the traditional "scientific" approach to research in that data are first collected and then common themes are identified and coded. The resulting categories are then used to formulate theory. Traditionally, a literature review isn't carried out beforehand as it may influence the coding process and therefore the theory.'

Sam's reflection

20 November

Grounded theory seemed great to me; no literature review. Well at least not until the end!

Whatever strategy I use I'll be looking at people's experiences and I suppose my definition of 'people' might be pupils in a class or teachers in a school , so if they have their own characteristics, maybe this is an ethnographic aspect to my research. Similarly, if I'm surely looking at their experience of events or phenomena, this could be a phenomenological aspect. And I may well try to construct some theory from the ground up after I collect my data. But while there may be aspects of all three in my research they're not my main strategies.

➡

I like the idea of action research but my research doesn't involve changing anything. I'm not planning any interventions. So it's not action research. It could be a case study. After all I have an 'instance' – children's fears/concerns and I am likely to do some interviews and maybe an observation or two. So I could claim that I have used multiple methods. Maybe it is a case study. Or it could be a survey. After all, most of my data will come from the questionnaires that I issue to the kids. The other data will only play a minor part in the final research

So how do I decide which it is? What was it that Richard said about case studies being detailed? Something about case studies being a three-dimensional picture of the instance. Will I be producing such a detailed picture? I don't think so. So it looks like I'll be doing a survey.

Record of tutorial

Student: Sam Sylon   **Date: 7/11/XX**
SUMMARY OF KEY LEARNING POINTS

- The research process can be envisaged as a three-tier hierarchical process. Level 1, the research methodology, deals with the underlying approach. Level 2, the research strategy, is about how the work will be structured – what vehicle will be used to undertake the work. Level 3 deals with the data collection tools.

- Case studies use multiple data collection methods to get a three-dimensional picture of the instance under review.

- It is essential to define both the nature of the instance and the boundaries of the case study.

- The instance may be one person or a group of people, an organisation or an event.

- Criteria used to choose the instance include interest, that it's typical or atypical, unique, extreme or convenient.
- Results from case studies are relatable but not generalisable.
- Evaluation criteria with other case studies could include similar time, place, people or organisation.
- Advantages of case studies include the use of multiple data collection methods, the ability to set boundaries and therefore the scale.
- Disadvantages include lack of generalisability, possible bias and the influence of the researcher.
- Action research is fundamentally self-reflective and collaborative, and often focussed on continuous professional development.
- Action research involves collecting baseline evidence, implementing an intervention which is continuously improved as a result of self-evaluation and finally producing an evaluation of the impact achieved by the intervention.
- Understanding of the approach varies and different models are prevalent. The key is to justify the approach in the context of your professional setting.
- Reflective diaries are often crucial to providing evidence of continuing development and evaluation. They should not be purely descriptive and they should include diverse sources of evidence.
- Advantages of action research include relevance to practice, diverse evidence and authenticity.
- Disadvantages include a tendency toward formulaic approaches, possible controversy and a lack of analytical rigour.
- Surveys involve canvassing the attitudes, opinions and demographics of a population usually using questionnaires, interviews, focus groups or observations.
- Surveys very often involve sampling only part of the population.
- Email surveys are growing in popularity.
- Questionnaires, interviews, focus groups and observations all have advantages and disadvantages in terms of aspects such as sample size, structured/unstructured, authenticity and bias.
- Fitness for purpose and readiness to evaluate your strategy is critical.

- A range of alternative approaches are available including:

  - ethnography, which involves studying people;

  - phenomenology, in which first-person experiences are studied;

  - grounded theory, which involves collecting and coding data, then formulating theory.

Agreed action points

Sam will:

- Review the research focus and questions and identify the most appropriate research strategy to adopt.

- Write a justification for the chosen strategy and compare this with the others, emphasising strengths and weaknesses in relation to the research focus.

- Evaluate the chosen strategy in terms of validity, reliability, ethics and bias.

A quick guide to deciding your research strategy

Question	Strategy

Do you intend to collect 80%+ of your data using only one data collection method? — Yes → A qualitative or quantitative survey depending on the nature of the research

No ↓

Will you be improving an aspect of professional practice by making a number of small interventions followed by data collection and evaluation? — Yes → An action research strategy

No ↓

Do you intend to use two or more data collection methods such as questionnaires, interviews and observations? — Yes → A qualitative and/or quantitative case study depending on the nature of the research

No ↓

Do you intend to undertake an controlled experiment or quasi-experiment? — Yes → A quantitative experiment

No ↓

Will you only use documentary data? — Yes → Documentary analysis

Additional information on the issues covered by this tutorial can be found at/in:

- www.pearsoned.co.uk/colesmcgrath
- **Denscombe, M.** (2008) *The Good Research Guide (3rd ed.).* McGraw Hill: Maidenhead, Chs. 1, 2, 8.
- **Cohen, L., Mannion, L. and Morrison, K.** (2007) *Research Methods in Education (6th ed.).* Routledge Falmer: London, Chs. 9, 11, 14.

GATHERING YOUR DATA – INTERVIEWS AND OBSERVATIONS

Aim of tutorial

In conjunction with Tutorial 7, to help you select and evaluate the most appropriate data collection tool/s for your research. Each method is described and evaluated.

Contents

→ How to organise an interview or observation

→ Shared characteristics of interviews and observations

→ Features of interviews

→ Writing interview questions

→ To record or take notes?

→ Features of observations

→ Participant and non-participant observations

22 November

At last! Today we'll be discussing something that I understand. No more research paradigms or research strategies. Instead, simple straightforward data collection methods. I think Richard is going to look at interviews, observations and questionnaires. I've used interviews and questionnaires in the past to collect data for assignments. I've also observed newly qualified teachers and peers and been observed by my line manager and colleagues. So there shouldn't be too many surprises, but then again Richard has a habit of looking at things from odd angles so I'd better not get overconfident.

Review of tutorial

Richard was surfing the Web when I entered. He looked up and waved me into a seat and logged off before saying, 'Hi, how are you?'

'Fine. I'm looking forward to today's session because at last it's something I have some experience of.'

'That's great. It's makes things easier if you have some practical experience of what we're discussing. What I want to look at is four common methods of data collection, namely interviews, observations, questionnaires and documentation. However, that's too much to cover in one tutorial so we'll look at interviews and observations today and have an extra tutorial next week to look at documentation and questionnaires. What methods have you used in the past?'

'I've used both interviews and questionnaires.'

'Excellent. But before we get into discussing the data collection methods, I want to talk a little bit about how you approach people that you want to collect data from. The first thing you have to remember is that they're doing you a favour, so treat them with consideration and respect. If I want to interview or observe someone I like to make personal contact with them and explain the purpose of my research before asking if they're willing to be involved. If they say "yes", I follow up my conversation with a detailed letter or email confirming the nature of the research and the conditions upon which they are taking part.'

'What would you include in your email?'

'After making initial contact to explain the research I'd contact those who had agreed to participate and confirm the date, time and venue of the interview or observation. You should always try to see the person on their "turf" not yours and if that is not possible use neutral ground.'

'I've read about this,' I said, 'It's a matter of putting them at their ease and limiting any fears or nerves that they might have.'

'Exactly! I'd follow that up by confirming that their anonymity will be protected at all times. Secondly, I would make it clear that they have the right to withdraw from the research at any stage up to the point when the final report is published. And finally I would explain to them how they could access my completed research.'

'So basically you pick up the main ethical issues and make sure that they understand the research and why they're taking part.'

'That's right.'

'Do you have an example of a letter that I could use?'

'There is one on my website **www.pearsoned.co.uk/colesmcgrath**.'

'Would you give them a copy of the interview or observation schedule in advance?'

'You have been reading up on this,' he said with a smile. 'I do like to provide my participants with a copy of any data collection instrument that I intend to use in advance. It gives them a chance to think about the type of issues that I'm interested in.'

'I asked because I'm not sure that it's a good idea. If you tell them what you're looking for it gives them a chance to prepare an answer or change their behaviour.'

'In theory that's true, but in reality people are too busy to prepare an answer in advance or to plan a change in their behaviour just for you. And the advantage is that it demonstrates that you are not trying to catch them out.'

'What about confidentiality?'

'I'm always cautious about promising confidentiality because I intend to write about what the people say and do. So it is difficult to claim that I'll treat what they reveal in confidence. That's why I emphasise anonymity. Of course during the interview or after the interview has ended people often tell you something "in confidence". And you can't divulge that unless you have a legal obligation, such as child protection issues. I once had a respondent who at the end of the interview said, "Now I'll tell you what I really think about the Principal" but I couldn't use it because it was told to me in confidence.'

Sam's reflection

23 November

I hadn't given much thought to the actual mechanics of arranging the interviews or observations. Previously, I'd just done things informally, but Richard wants me to include a copy of any formal communication that I have with my respondents as an appendix. When you think about it he's right. This module is all about learning how to do a small-scale piece of research, so I need to provide evidence of what I've done and how I've done it. And that includes the management and organisation of the project. In addition, if I'm ever involved in a large-scale research project I'll have to deal with these issues, so I might as well get some practice in now.

I agree with what Richard says about confidentiality. But I'm not so sure about sending the interview questions to the respondents in advance. I know several people who would think about their answers if they knew what the questions were going to be and most teachers I know change their teaching approach when they know they're being observed.

Review of tutorial

'The first thing I want to stress is that the type of interviews and observations that you use can be plotted on a continuum that runs from highly structured to completely unstructured.'

'And in the middle you have semi-structured,' I suggested.

'Exactly. In a completely structured interview you'd have a long list of questions such as, name, age, gender, job title, length of time in present post, educational experience, etcetera. and be very specific about what you ask.'

'But that's more like a questionnaire than an interview,' I said.

'True. But it is an interview because you are sitting in front of the person asking the questions. It would be described as highly structured because as the interviewer you've decided the parameters of the discussion in advance and the type of question you're asking requires specific information from the respondent that ensures that they can't digress from your agenda.'

'That sounds like one very boring interview.'

'It probably is, but it can be used with young children or any respondent who might have difficulty completing a questionnaire. At the other end of the continuum you have the completely unstructured interview where you sit down with someone and say something like "Tell me about your experience as a teacher." That's a very open question and it invites the respondent to tell you whatever they think is important about their experiences.'

I didn't like the sound of that. I had visions of growing old as someone told me their life story in stultifying detail. 'I'm not keen on that as a type of interview either.'

'Very few small-scale research projects use this approach because of the time it takes to carry out and analyse a series of unstructured interviews.'

'I think I prefer semi-structured interviews.'

'Most people do. Semi-structured interviews sit in the middle of the continuum. But before we discuss interviews in a bit more detail, I'd like to emphasise that the same range of options applies to observations. You can have observations where you could go into a classroom with a highly detailed schedule of actions that you expect to observe and as you see each action you would place a tick next to the appropriate box. Or you could just go in with a blank sheet of paper and record anything that caught your attention. Both data collection approaches share the same common underlying structure. Here, this handout should clarify what I am saying.'

Sam's reflection

23 November

I don't like the idea of either highly structured or highly unstructured data collection instruments. Structured approaches only allow you to collect data on issues that you've identified in advance. Effectively, you'd be saying that you already know what all the important issues are. How would you find out if something important was going on that you hadn't identified? However, the unstructured approach involves collecting loads of data, much of which might be irrelevant. Not to mention that it would take forever to analyse. No, I'll stick with my semi-structured approach.

Review of tutorial

'So let's look at interviews in a bit more detail. When would you use interviews as a method of data collection?'

'When I need to find out people's views on an issue,' I said confidently.

'If that is all you want to do why not use a questionnaire? After all it would be easier and you could send it to more people than you could reasonably interview?'

'True, but you use interviews when you want to explore people's attitudes or beliefs in depth. It would be hard to do that using a questionnaire.'

'True. You use interviews when you want to dig into people's attitudes, beliefs, feelings or perceptions. Interviews provide a depth of information that you just can't get from a questionnaire.'

'I understand that, but looking at your handout (*see below*) I don't think that structured interviews would give you that kind of data and open-ended interviews would take forever.'

'As I've said, that's why most single researchers use semi-structured interviews. The researcher knows the broad areas that they wish to collect information on and so they ask a series of open-ended questions. The use of open-ended questions allows the respondent to express their own views on the issue. If they start to digress too much the researcher can pull them back by asking a supplementary question or saying something like "that's an interesting observation on the Governors' Christmas party but could you tell me a little more about how you deal with misbehaving children?"'

'So you've heard about our Governors' Christmas party?' I said laughing. 'But if semi-structured interviews are so useful what's the point of structured and unstructured interviews?'

'As I said, the structured interview can be used instead of a questionnaire when you're dealing with children or people who either can't read or understand a questionnaire or with any group that are likely to give a poor response rate. In a way what you're doing is delivering a questionnaire personally. The unstructured interview is really useful when you're investigating a new topic and want to find out about the major themes and ideas contained within it. They're particularly valuable when you're undertaking an in-depth study of people's experiences over an extended period of time, for example their experiences at school. However, they take up a lot of time as issues are explored in depth and the data analysis can be a nightmare.'

'So the type of interview that you conduct is determined by what you want to find out and the people that you intend to interview.'

'Correct. But you also have to take into account the time that you have available and the word limit on your assignment. You have to be practical. Think of the Goldilocks theory (Davis 2007). The structured interviews are too small, like Baby Bear's bed: they may not produce enough data for many small-scale projects. The unstructured interview is the equivalent of Daddy Bears bed: they may take too much time and produce too much data. But the semi-structured interview is just right, like Mummy Bear's bed.'

Sam's reflection

24 November

I can't believe that my lecturer has just used Goldilocks and the Three Bears to explain a concept in research theory. I bet if I told the tabloid papers there would be an outcry about the dumbing-down of education.

But the truth is I think it is a good example which I need to apply to all aspects of my research. The number of words I have available limits the amount of literature I can include, the number of data collection tools I can use and the number of people I can collect data from. I need to be selective in choosing my sources too. Similarly, with the amount of data I collect — there is only so much I can report and analyse in my findings. It's quality not quantity that I need to go for. I must be selective.

Review of tutorial

'How would you suggest that I go about deciding on my interview questions?' I asked. 'I've always found this difficult.'

'This is really important. It's often the case that we see questions that have a very loose link with the research questions and this is a problem as clearly appropriate answers won't be obtained. Start by looking at your research questions. Take each one in turn and try to break them down into various themes. This will give you a list of words or phrases that you can use to formulate your initial interview questions. Write these out. When you've finished look at your list of possible interview questions and eliminate duplicate questions. Then look and see if any questions can be amalgamated. Only after you have done this do you want to start editing the questions.'

'You mean check your questions as you do with a questionnaire?'

'Precisely. Check that your questions are unambiguous and that you've not asked any leading questions.'

'You mean like, "would you agree with me that . . ."'

'Exactly. You want the interviewees' views and therefore you must do everything you can to avoid influencing their answers. This includes thinking carefully about the order in which you ask the questions.'

'Why would the order be important?'

'Sometimes the order of the questions can lead the interviewee in a particular direction. For example once Dorothy was on the "yellow brick road" she was led inexorably to Oz. You can do the same thing with your participants if you aren't careful.'

I knew that Richard wouldn't be able to provide an exact answer to my next question but I asked it anyway. 'In a 25/30-minute semi-structured interview how many questions should I ask?'

'That's like asking "how long is a piece of string?" I would suggest that five or six is the maximum. After all, they have to be broad enough to encourage the person to express their views in some detail.'

'And the first question should be used to put them at their ease?'

'Yes, but don't ask a question that has little bearing on your research. That's just a waste of your time. So ask an easy question that is relevant.'

'OK, but how many interviews do I need to do?'

'We're back to that piece of string again. In reality you conduct as many interviews as are necessary to answer your research questions. But usually for a 5000-word assignment I would say four should be sufficient.'

'Of course!' I said remembering one of the early tutorials. 'You said that an average 30-minute interview produced four or five sheets of A4 single spaced transcript. So four interviews would produce 16 pages or 8000 words and the findings section of my 7500 word assignment will only be about 3000 words.'

'So it might be that you could get away with three half-hour interviews or four 20/25-minute interviews. But your decision must be based on collecting enough useful data to answer your research questions. It is a matter of judgement.'

Sam's reflection

24 November

First 'Goldilocks', now the 'Wizard of Oz', what next, Cinderella? Still it was good advice to analyse my research questions as the first stage in writing my interview questions. That way I can make sure that they relate directly to my research questions. I suppose drawing up an interview schedule is a bit like dancing. We can all move about on the dance floor but the trained dancer really does stand out as does a good interview schedule.

What Richard said about the number of questions seems sensible. Basically he's allowing five minutes for the person to answer a question.

There's something nagging at the back of my mind about research questions and their link to interview questions. What is it?

Got it! Once I've written my interview questions I need to check that they're capable of producing the data I need to answer each of my research questions and that I haven't missed anything in the editing. I can do this by drawing up a list of my research questions and a list of the interview questions side by side and linking them together with lines showing which interview question helps answer which research question, maybe like this:

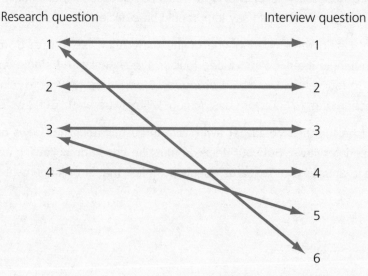

What I must avoid is the situation where I ask an interview question that has no links with my research questions. If I do that I'm just wasting time. BUT what is even more important is that I don't end up with a research question that has no links to any of my interview questions. If that happens it means that I wouldn't have any data to answer that question! I think my diagram is really useful, I wonder if Richard uses something similar.

Review of tutorial

'Do I need to tape and transcribe every interview that I undertake?' I asked.

'That is a difficult question to answer. I think best practice would suggest that you tape and transcribe every interview. However, there are problems with such an approach. For example, not everyone likes to be recorded and if your subject refuses to be taped you have to respect their decision. But if your respondent is happy to be taped you still need to decide if you're going to transcribe the whole tape or just those sections that you're particularly interested in. If you cherry-pick "the best sections" to transcribe you run the risk of ignoring data which appears boring but is actually important. A full transcription of a 30-minute interview takes time – maybe two or three hours so you have to weigh the advantages and dis-advantages of your approach.'

'But some people just take notes when interviewing, is that poor practice?'

'It depends. Each researcher has to justify the approach they take. So if the researcher believed that the use of a recorder would distract the respondent and cause them to censor their answers she might decide to take notes in the meeting or to write up her notes of the meeting immediately after the interview.'

'I would have thought that it would be better to take notes in the meeting.'

'Possibly, but while you are taking notes you are not concentrating on what the person is saying. This can distract the interviewee and you may fail to pick up on body language or something important.'

'This interviewing business isn't easy,' I said

'No it isn't. Interviewing is a skill and like any other skill it has to be learnt and the only way you can improve is through practice. Remember you want to find out what the respondent thinks or feels about an issue, so you need to let them do the talking and through your body language make it clear that you are actively listening to them. Most people like to be asked for their opinion and will welcome the opportunity to expound their views. However, don't get into a discussion with them and tell them what you think even if they ask for your views. Side-step such requests by saying "we can talk about my views later". Just ask your questions and give the interviewee the time and space to respond. Don't be impatient with them and jump in to fill silences and never argue or appear shocked by anything they say. Instead, encourage them to expand on issues of interest by saying something like "that's very interesting could you tell me a little bit more about it".'

'You said previously that I don't need to include copies of each transcript as an appendix when I submit my work . . .'

'Some colleges and universities require you to do this. But all I want to see is a blank copy of the interview schedule.'

I breathed a sigh of relief at this and muttered 'good' under my breath. Glad to have this confirmed.

Sam's reflection

25 November

I'm still not a 100 per cent sure that I'll use interviews. But if I do I think that I'll record and transcribe each one. It will take a bit of time but once I have the full transcripts in front of me I'll be able to compare and contrast what each interviewee said on every question. I'll also be able to do searches using F5 in Word to find specific words and phrases across each script. Of course if my interviewees don't want to be recorded I'll have to take notes.

Review of tutorial

'So if you use interviews to find out what people say they do why do we need observations?' asked Richard.

'Because people don't always do what they say they do,' I ventured.

'Precisely! Very often people are unaware that there's a difference between what they say and what they actually do. For example, it is not unusual for a teacher to describe their teaching style as learner-centred. But when you observe them teach they might use teacher-centred methods most of the time. Therefore, to find out what is actually happening you need to do some observations.'

'Are you saying teachers are self-delusional?' I asked with malicious glee.

'No', he smiled. 'I'm saying everyone is delusional. None of us ever really know how we and our actions are perceived by other people.'

'That sounds like my Head. But surely it is hard to get people to act naturally if they know they're being observed?'

'That's true, but there are two types of observation, **participative** and **non-participative**. An OfSTED inspector who sits at the back of the class watching you teach is using non-participative observation. They're alien to the classroom and don't take part in the lesson. Their presence changes the behaviour of both the teacher and the children.'

'It certainly changes mine!,' I said.

Richard laughed and then continued. 'Participant observation occurs when the researcher collects data at the same time as they engage in their normal activities. For example, a teacher might be teaching a class, but she may also be observing how learners react to certain teaching methods. She doesn't record her findings in the class but waits until the end of the lesson and then writes her notes up.'

'What you're saying is that she carries out her observations in secret without telling anyone and that way people act normally.'

'Not really. Remember that one of the cardinal ethical requirements is that you obtain informed consent. So if you want to conduct participant observation on a group of learners or teachers you have to ask their permission to do so.'

'But wouldn't that defeat the whole purpose of participant observation. The respondent would know that you are looking at them and act differently,' I argued.

'Well the way I get round that is to explain the purpose of my research and ask the participants if I can observe them as part of my project. If they agree, I then leave it for a week or two before I do the observation. By then they've forgotten about my research and have reverted to acting normally.'

'That's a bit sneaky isn't it?'

'**Not really.**' He said with a smile that said butter wouldn' t melt in his mouth. 'I've obtained their informed consent and explained what I intend to do, so I'm not deceiving them.'

Sam's reflection

25 November

I quite like the idea of participant observation. It allows me to act out my spy fantasies and observe people without them knowing. It's probably the best way of capturing what people actually do. They don't realise or have forgotten that they're being watched and so they act more naturally than they would in an interview or a non-participant observation. I could make a note of what they say too. I would imagine that if done properly you could collect some really good data from participant observations. Mind you, you'd probably have to do a number of observations over a period of time to gather sufficient data.

Review of tutorial

'From what you say it sounds as if non-participant observers are likely to use observation checklists prepared in advance.'

'I think that's probably right. The non-participant observer is more likely to use a checklist to record what they see. For example, they might have a category "child asks teacher a question". Every time this occurs they would place a tick against that activity. At the end of the session they would add up the number of ticks and be able to report that on 13 occasions a child asked the teacher a question.'

'Does this mean that a researcher using participant observation is likely to use unstructured observations?'

'Participant observers are unlikely to use a written schedule but that doesn't mean that they haven't got a list of items to look out for in their mind. The participant observer will have considered what actions or activities are relevant to their research in advance and will look for these. During the observation they may make the odd rough note to remind them of what they've observed or heard, but it is more likely that they'll find a few minutes after the observation to jot down some notes. Unlike the structured observation they wouldn't be able to specify the number of times a learner asked a question of the teacher but they would be able to say something like, "the children regularly asked the teacher questions."'

'So they would write up what they saw as a series of notes and use that as the record of data collected?'

'Or they could write up their observations in the form of a reflective journal. This is a really useful approach because it allows the researcher to reflect upon and become engaged with the events observed. They can then interpret them at their leisure.'

'Do you have any examples of interview or observation schedules that I could look at?'

'Yes of course. You will find them on my website **www.pearsoned.co.uk/coles mcgrath**.'

Sam's reflection

25 November

From what Richard has said I think that I prefer semi-structured observations. But observations are not going to play much of a part in my current research. I want to know what the children think. I can't ➡

find that out by just watching them. Any data I collect would be based on my interpretation of what I'd seen. For example if a child looked concerned about going home I wouldn't know if that was because they were afraid of the journey or because they were worried about what was waiting for them . A ping moment – I could use what I have just written to justify my rejection of observations!

Record of tutorial

Student Sam Sylon   **Date: 22/11/XX**
SUMMARY OF KEY LEARNING POINTS

- When arranging interviews and observations follow up any initial contact with participants with an email or letter.
- Confirm date, time and venue in writing.
- In order to address ethical issues include statements in the letter/email concerning anonymity, the participant's right to withdraw at any time and details of how they can access the final report/results.
- Consider sending the participants a copy of the interview or observation schedule in advance.
- Both observations and interviews can be located on a spectrum that runs from highly structured to totally unstructured.
- Interviews are used to collect data on peoples' attitudes, beliefs, feelings and opinions.
- The type of interview used depends on how much you know about the subject and the abilities of respondents.
- It is vital to refer to the research questions when drawing up the interview questions and the observation schedule. Use a chart to confirm that the interview or observation schedule will collect the data required to answer the research questions.

- Consider how to record the interview – tape record or take notes. When deciding what approach to take, think about analysis of data collected.
- Observations reveal what people do, they do not explain why they act in a particular manner.
- When using observations consider which method of observation is most suitable – participant or non-participant observation? The choice depends on what the researcher already knows, what they want to find out and the attitudes of the respondents.
- Consider how to record observations – use detailed schedules, notes written-up during or after the observation or a reflective journal.

Agreed action points

Sam will:

- Decide if interviews and questionnaires or just questionnaires are to be used in the research.
- Review the example letter to participants on my website www.pearsoned.co.uk/colesmcgrath and draft a covering letter to accompany any questionnaire or interview schedule that may be used.
- Check that the intended data collection tool/s (interview schedule/observation schedule/questionnaire) is capable of collecting the data required to answer all research questions.

Collecting the data – interviews and observations

Your research focus and questions determine the type and content of the data that you collect

↓

Map the data that you need to answer your research questions

Are you concerned with attitudes, beliefs, feelings or perceptions of people, or why they behave in a certain way?

←— No —→

Are you concerned with what people do?

Yes

Yes

Interviews

Strengths

- Allows in-depth exploration
- Can respond to the direction of discussion
- Guaranteed response
- Format can be varied, e.g. face-to-face/ telephone

Weaknesses

- Time-consuming
- Only small samples possible
- Can be difficult to analyse
- Bias can be problematic

Observations

Strengths

- Authentic/naturalistic
- Varied format – structured/unstructured/ participant/non- participant
- Varied data collection – audio/video

Weaknesses

- Bias an issue whether participant or non- participant
- Analysis can be complex
- Time-consuming

Handout

CONTINUUM OF INTERVIEWS AND OBSERVATIONS

Approach	Examples	Strengths	Weaknesses
Highly structured: The researcher determines in advance what information they wish to collect.	Questions/ categories are pre-specified in detail and allow for only specific answers, e.g. yes, no, age, agree, disagree, behaviour seen/not seen, count.	Data analysis is simplified.	The researcher's view of what is important dominates data collected and restrains respondent from expressing their views.
Semi-structured: The researcher knows the broad headings that they wish to collect data on but is open to the unexpected provided it is broadly relevant to their research.	Questions/ categories are broader. Questions and observation prompts are seen as starting point for the collection of data rather than the end.	Reduced researcher bias. The respondents' actions or words are used to determine what is important. This increases the likelihood that data new to the researcher will be uncovered.	Increased variability in the issues covered leading to increased problems of comparability and data analysis.
Unstructured: The researcher has an interest in a particular issue but does not wish to limit the research to parameters that they impose either arbitrarily or because of their lack of knowledge.	Questions are broad and open ended. Observation schedules may be 'blank' or composed of just a few prompts.	Researcher bias is minimised and the range of issues identified expanded very significantly.	Comparability between data sets is significantly increased making analysis much more difficult and time-consuming.

Additional information on the issues covered by this tutorial can be found at/in:

- www.pearsoned.co.uk/colesmcgrath
- **Cohen, L., Mannion, L. and Morrison, K.** (2007) *Research Methods in Education (6th ed.).* Routledge Falmer: London, Chs.16, 18.
- **Denscombe, M.** (2008) *The Good Research Guide (3rd ed.).* McGraw Hill: Maidenhead, Ch.10.
- **Newby, P.** (2010) *Research Methods for Education.* Longman, Pearson: Harlow, Ch.9.

GATHERING YOUR DATA – DOCUMENTS AND QUESTIONNAIRES

Aim of tutorial

In conjunction with Tutorial 6, to help you select and evaluate the most appropriate data collection tool/s for your research. Each method is described and evaluated.

Contents

→ Use of documents as data

→ Critical review of documents used as data

→ Types of questionnaires

→ Types of questions

→ Checking the questionnaire

→ Communicating with your respondents

→ Improving response rates

Sam's reflection

29 November

I've had a busy week trying to review last week's tutorial tape, write up my notes and prepare for today's session. Still the course is almost over. Now's not the time to slow down. We're looking at questionnaires and documentation today. It should be really useful as I am fairly sure that I'll use questionnaires as my main data collection tool. I think I'll issue them to all children aged 7 to 11 in my school. That will give me much more coverage than I could ever achieve if I were to interview them. What I'm not so sure about is what does Richard mean by documentation? When we last talked about documentation it was with reference to the literature review. Unless he's on about statistics such as exam and SATs results.

Review of tutorial

Richard was reading a book when I entered. He appeared to be scribbling notes in the margin.

'I hope that's not a library book,' I said, trying to tease him.

'No. It's a book which I have been asked to review. I find that I understand things better if I engage with a book and have a conversation with the author about their ideas rather than just passively absorb what they have to say. You should try it.'

'So you must be one of those people who like second-hand books that people have written notes in?'

'Only if the writing is neat! But enough of this idle chit-chat, you're here to work,' he said in his best imitation of a grumpy old man. 'Today I want to look at questionnaires and documentation as sources of data. We've already looked at the use of diverse sources for your literature review, but some sources can also provide data for your findings. What type of documents do you think you could use for data in a research report?'

'I've been thinking about this. Previously you said that I could include documents and reports from the Government, the TDA, OfSTED, the local education authority and my school in the literature review. So I assume that the type of documentary data that goes in the findings would be restricted to statistics on achievement and suchlike.'

'That's interesting. I did say that official reports and documentation could be used in the literature review. Very often such documents are used to contextualise the issues that you're looking at, to place them in a broader picture. But the content of official documents can also be used as data and not just the statistics contained in them. For example, if the focus of your research was the impact of school inspections on teachers you might well include data and comments from various OfSTED reports. In reality what determines if a particular document is used as a source of literature or data is the focus of your research. Do you understand?'

'I think so,' I said doubtfully.

'Let me give you an example from your own research. you're looking at children's perceptions of their safety at school. You could use a government report on parents' perceptions of their child's safety at school in your literature review to contextualise the issues you want to explore. But if the school had already produced a report on how parents of children in the school felt about safety you could use that as a source of data for your project.'

'So, what you're saying is that the focus of your research determines if you use a particular document as literature or data.'

'Sometimes as both in the same report! However, you're right when you say that official documents are often used as a source of statistical data. For example, if you wanted to compare your school's performance against the local, regional or national averages on a whole range of measures then a chat with your Head, local education advisor or a search of Google Scholar will more than likely reveal a whole raft of statistical reports and returns that you could use. The UK Statistics Authority and the Organisation for Economic Co-operation and Development (OECD) are all useful sources.'

'But you said that I should be critical of everything I read. So how much reliance can I put on data in any official report and the data in it?'

'That's a really good point. What I think I said was that you need to critically evaluate every source that you use. Churchill once said that "there are lies, damn lies and statistics". So you need to know at least two things about any set of statistics before you rely on them. Firstly, how were they calculated and secondly, for what purpose were they calculated. To give you an idea of how statistics can be warped to support any argument I remember a newspaper headline not so long ago which read "Fifty percent of all schools are below average". What makes you think that the writer was a critic of the Government's education policy?'

'But that sort of bias would also apply to reports that contained few or no statistics.'

'Absolutely! As I say, the golden rule in research is to critically evaluate every document and piece of information you rely on for data or literature and think about the motives that the authors might have for taking a particular view. Remember provenance. Of course, there are practical limits to how far you can take this approach. It would be impossible to carry out a minute and detailed scrutiny of every document that you use. What you want to do is cultivate a critical and enquiring mindset. You need to ask yourself if, based on the evidence available, the claims made in the document are reasonable.'

Sam's reflection

30 November

I'm still not entirely certain that I understand the difference between documents that I use as data and documents that I include in my literature review. Let's think how I can distinguish the two. This requires a cup of tea and a fig roll.

I suppose the easiest way to decide is to ask, 'does this document contain data that directly helps me to answer one or more of my research questions?' If it does then it is data. If it only contains data that contextualises the issues I'm looking at, or which I use to explore and challenge the data I've collected then it's literature. That's not bad as a rough guide.

Review of tutorial

'Right let's talk about questionnaires. Last time we said that interviews and observations could be located on a continuum from highly structured to completely unstructured. Well questionnaires can also fit onto that continuum. You could have a highly structured questionnaire that only asked closed questions such as age, gender, etcetera or you could have one that asked people to write about their views on a particular subject.'

'I don't think that you'd get many responses from a totally unstructured questionnaire, it would take too long to complete,' I said.

'And that is why you very seldom see an unstructured questionnaire. Research seems to indicate that if a postal questionnaire can't be completed in six to eight minutes most people throw it in the bin. Of course if you give your respondents some inducement such as entry into a prize draw or free shopping vouchers people may be willing to spend longer on the task.'

'But surely, if I give the questionnaire to colleagues or my learners they would be willing to spend longer completing it?'

'You'd think so, but I wouldn't bet on it. They get bored and you don't want to annoy them with long-winded and poorly designed questionnaires remember . . .'

'I know,' I interrupted. 'They're doing me a favour, so I need to keep my questionnaire short and snappy.'

'Correct. But that doesn't mean that you can only ask closed questions. A well designed questionnaire can contain a mixture of open and closed questions. So you tell me what sort of questions might appear on a questionnaire?'

'You can have closed questions such as name, gender, date of birth. Multiple choice questions where you just tick the correct one. Then there are those where you are asked to ring those words that apply to you and of course there are the Likert-scale questions where you say if you agree strongly, agree, neither agree or disagree, disagree and disagree strongly . . .'

'That's pretty good. You could ask people to rank things in order of preference too, for example. This handout lists the most common type of questions used and gives you an example of each. There are further examples on my website **www.pearsoned.co.uk/colesmcgrath**. What you need to do is decide what information you need to collect and select the right type of question to elicit that information. What this means in practice is that most good questionnaires contain a variety of question types. So how do you check that your questionnaire is going to collect the information that you need?'

Now was the time to tell him about my idea of listing my research questions and linking them directly to questions or observation categories on my data collection tool. 'Here it's easier if I show you,' I said and quickly drafted out my idea. 'What I'd do is list both my research questions and those contained in the questionnaire and then draw lines to indicate which questions help answer my research questions.'

'That's very good. Where did you get that idea from?'

'It was something that came to me when I was reviewing our last tutorial.'

'Well it's a really good idea. Do you mind if I pinch it for my other students?'

'No, not at all,' I said feeling pleased. Clearly it's not just the experts who can come up with a good idea.

'Once you've confirmed that you're collecting the data you need to answer your research questions, what do you need to do with the questionnaire?'

'I've always been told that you must pilot a questionnaire,' I said.

'Correct. And who should you pilot the questionnaire with?'

'Well I'd give it to a colleague first and ask them to check it for use of English and clarity of meaning. That way I could pick up on any questions that were ambiguous. Then I'd amend it in the light of any feedback that they gave me and only then would I pilot it with a representative sample of my intended participants.'

'I can see that you've done this before. I like the idea of getting the questionnaire checked by a colleague and don't forget that you can also run it past your hardworking supervisor. I would also ask the colleague to look out for any compound questions that you might have missed. These can be difficult to spot. I remember asking the question "on a scale of 1 to 5, with 5 being excellent how would you describe management and leadership in the school?" The problem was that while management and leadership are linked concepts they are not the same, and you could have good management but poor leadership. So I was unable to use the answers to that question in my report because I didn't know if the respondents were grading the school's management or leadership. But why give it to participants if a colleague has checked it?'

'Just because a colleague understands your questionnaire doesn't mean that a child or parent will. Teachers use a lot of jargon and although my colleague would understand it my intended participants might not. I also need to check how long it takes a participant to complete the questionnaire.'

'Very good. Questionnaires are hard to design. They take a lot more time to develop than a set of interview questions. But once completed they are comparatively easy to analyse.'

'Do I need a computer package to analyse my questionnaire?'

'The value of most packages on offer is that they can perform various statistical calculations for you. However, the difficulty is usually choosing which statistical test to use. Sometimes samples in small-scale projects can be so small that statistically significant results are unobtainable. The data from most small-scale research projects can be analysed manually or by using Excel. Of course if you intend to use questionnaires frequently, you might consider looking at questionnaire design and analysis software such as SNAP or SurveyMonkey. Both are available in our IT suites and most colleges and universities offer access to similar packages. If you're considering using them in the future you should Google them for more information. We'll be talking more about analysis of data in a couple of week's time. So all I'll say now is that as you design your questionnaire give some thought to how you will analyse your results. Many students only think about this after they have collected their data and this can cause problems.'

'OK,' I said. As Richard shifted in his chair I piped up with a question that had been on my mind. 'I know what you're going to say but I'm going to ask anyway. How many questionnaires do I need returned for my project?'

'You know me so well,' he said smiling. 'As you rightly guessed, you need as many questionnaires returned as are required to answer your research questions. What you really need is enough relevant and interesting data to fill your findings section. What is certain is that if you send the questionnaire by post or email you will not get a 100 per cent response. Typically the response rate on postal questionnaires is around 22 per cent. Obviously this is higher when you send the questionnaire to people you know. The best return rate is when you have a captive audience and participants complete the questionnaire while you are present, for example when you collect data from your own class. However, we come back to the question of informed consent. You shouldn't use your position to force anyone to fill in a questionnaire.'

'How can I improve the response rate?'

'We spoke last time about the importance of explaining to people the purpose of your research and the basis upon which they take part in it. If you're asking strangers to fill in a postal or email questionnaire then the importance of this communication increases significantly. A well written request will increase the return rate. What do you think should go in such a letter?'

Unless it was a trick question the answer seemed obvious. 'It would cover the same issues as the letter or email you send to people you're going to interview or observe. So it would talk about anonymity, the fact that completion of the questionnaire isn't compulsory and how participants can get a copy of the final report. All those sort of things.'

'Good. You've clearly got the right idea. If you want to see an example of the kind of letter that can accompany a questionnaire go to my website **www. pearsoned.co.uk/colesmcgrath**. You should also enclose a stamped addressed envelope if it's a postal questionnaire. To improve response rates you can think about sending a polite follow-up letter or email to non-responders. But don't deluge the person with reminders, it will only irritate them. One reminder is sufficient. And don't, whatever you do, design a questionnaire that takes ages to complete.'

Sam's reflection

1 December

This was a short tutorial. Why Richard didn't tag it on to the end of last week's session I don't know. Maybe he thought it was too much for me to grasp in one session. Or perhaps he wanted to get off to a match or another salsa lesson. Who knows?

Perhaps because I've used questionnaires before I found the session fairly easy. Or maybe I'm just gaining in confidence. Certainly I feel a lot more confident about my ability to carry out a small-scale piece of research than when I started. I'd be in trouble if I didn't! But I think it's more than that. I think I'm beginning to see that certain principles underpin all research, such as clarity of aims, transparency concerning what I have done and how I have done it, criticality and a genuine concern for the wellbeing of my respondents.

What Richard didn't mention is how questionnaires need to be designed with the needs and abilities of respondents in mind. I know from past experience that you can't give the same questionnaire to young children as you would adults. The questionnaire has to be designed with the participant in mind. That's why I'm going to use a range of faces, from smiling to frowning, in my Likert questions. Faces will mean more to the younger children than words. One thing the session has done is confirm that I intend to use questionnaires as my main data collection source.

What I now have to decide is do I send the questionnaires to all the children aged 7–11 or just a sample?

Record of tutorial

Student: Sam Sylon   **Date: 29/11/XX**
SUMMARY OF KEY LEARNING POINTS

- Documentation can be used as either literature or data.
- Documentation that contextualises the issues or which is used to explain, explore and challenge findings is likely to be literature.
- Documents that contain information which help answer the research questions can be used as a source of data.
- Whether official documents are used as literature or a source of data it is

➡

necessary to critically evaluate the material, e.g. for what purpose were they written? How was the data collected? Has the data been independently verified?

- Questionnaires must be accompanied by a letter or email explaining the purpose of the research, the respondents' right to refuse to take part in the research and the conditions that will apply should they take part.

- A good questionnaire will be clearly presented, unambiguous and relatively quick to complete (no more than 8 minutes). To achieve this a peer and/or supervisor should review the questionnaire prior to it being piloted with potential participants.

- A range of different types of questions can be used to collect the data required to answer research questions (see handout).

- Keep in mind the age, ability and level of understanding of respondents when designing the questionnaire. Try to make them as attractive as possible.

- Consider how you will sample your population and how you will maximise the response rate.

Agreed action points

Sam will:

- Design a questionnaire suitable for children aged 7–11 in the school.

- Have a colleague review the questionnaire before sending it to me for comment.

- Amend questionnaire in light of comments received and pilot it with one child from each year group.

- Draft covering letter to accompany questionnaire.

Collecting the data – questionnaires

TYPES OF QUESTIONS FOUND IN A QUESTIONNAIRE

Question Type	Example
Closed	Please state your: Name Age Gender
Range questions	Please indicate how old you are: 20–29, 30–39, 40–49, 50–59, 60 and over. *(Note: Don't make the following common mistake. Please indicate how old you are:* *20–30, 30–40, 40–50 etc.)*
Multiple choice questions	Which of the following statements is untrue. Tick one only: During the 1970s Margaret was the Minister for Education. ❑ Margaret Thatcher was forced to resign as Prime Minister when she failed to defeat decisively Michael Heseltine when he stood for leadership of the Conservative Party in 1990. ❑ Tony Blair succeeded Margaret Thatcher as Prime Minister in 1997. ❑
Ranking	Rank the following teaching methods in terms of your personal preference, with one being your favourite. ❑ Lecture ❑ group work ❑ pair working ❑ role play ❑ team teaching ❑ discussion ❑ discovery learning ❑ student presentations
Select	Ring each of the following teaching methods that you use on a regular basis (i.e. once per week). Lecture ❑ group work ❑ pair working ❑ role play ❑ discussion ❑ discovery learning ❑ student presentations ❑

Question Type	Example
Likert scale	Read the following sentence and circle the statement that best describes your reaction: OfSTED inspections help teachers to improve their professional practice. Agree strongly ❏ agree ❏ neither agree or disagree ❏ disagree ❏ disagree strongly ❏.
Semi-structured	*Typically semi-structured questions ask you to write a short comment on your answer to the previous question.*
Unstructured	*Such questions are rarely used but typically they ask the respondent to write a paragraph in response to the question posed.*

Additional information on the issues covered by this tutorial can be found at/in:

- www.pearsoned.co.uk/colesmcgrath
- OECD – http://www.oecd.org
- Cohen, L., Mannion, L. and Morrison, K. (2007) *Research Methods in Education (6th ed.).* Routledge Falmer: London, Chs.8, 15.
- Denscombe, M. (2008) *The Good Research Guide (3rd ed.).* McGraw Hill: Maidenhead, Chs.10, 12.
- Newby, P. (2010) *Research Methods for Education.* Longman, Pearson: Harlow, Chs. 9,10.

ANALYSIS OF QUALITATIVE DATA

Aim of tutorial

To enable you to analyse, evaluate and report qualitative data. A step by step approach guides you through the process of comparing and contrasting data, including making links with the theories contained in your literature review.

Contents

→ The need to code data

→ Elements of a coding system

→ Cutting and pasting themes and issues

→ Using quotes from data collected

→ Timing of analysis

→ Presentation of data:
  – Discursive
  – Tables
  – Diagrams

Sam's reflection

13 December

Tonight is the last session before we break up for Christmas. I'll be glad of the rest. But it will also give me a chance to catch up on my reading. Now that I have a pretty good idea of research terminology I'm starting to find that I can make more sense of the various books that Richard has recommended. Looking around the library last week I found dozens of books on research. I wonder what sort of sad individual spends a year writing a book on research methodology. They really do need to get a life.

Review of tutorial

Richard was tidying his desk when I entered. Old magazines, minutes of meetings and handouts overflowed from the waste bin and formed a large pool of type on the floor.

'It's my annual clear-out,' he said grinning. 'Once a year I throw out every document that I haven't used in the past 12 months, or which I am unlikely to use in the next year. It has a great liberating effect – especially just before Christmas. Now hang on while I put this lot in the recycle bin.'

I sat down and set up the tape.

Richard returned, slightly out of breath with a faint line of perspiration on his upper lip. 'Right,' he said, 'Analysis of qualitative data. Remember when I said that interviews, observations and questionnaires all resided on a continuum that ran from structured to unstructured?'

'Yes,' I nodded.

'Well when it comes to the analysis of qualitative data many of the same principles, processes and procedures apply whether we are looking at data from interviews, observations or questionnaires. So what we will do is look at the analysis of an interview transcript first and then consider what additional elements come into play when dealing with questionnaires and observation schedule.'

'OK, but remember that I'm most interested in questionnaires.'

'Understood. The first thing you have to do is code the data. Even if you use a computer package you will have to provide a code to identify each element of data that you may wish to comment on. Therefore you have to think about a coding system.'

'I hate codes. Every time I want to order a batch of paper I have to fill in another requisition form and supply an accounts code that was designed to be imposs- ible to remember.'

'Well in that case make sure your coding system is simple and memorable.'

'Such as?' I asked.

'Let's assume that you interview four teachers about their views on child safety. You record the interviews and transcribe them. First step, take a photocopy of transcription one and go through it with a highlighter pen. Highlight any words, ideas, events, issues or comments that you think are significant or interesting. Include any issues that you hadn't previously thought about. Then do the same for transcripts two to four. Leave a gap between each session of analysis. Avoid as far as possible any tendency to consciously look for the same issues that you identified previously. And don't ignore the mundane and apparently boring for the sake of the unusual and exciting.'

'But what about the coding?' I asked.

'I'm coming to that. Take transcript one. We can call it teacher one or transcript one. Either way, the first part of your code is T1. The second part relates to the page number on the transcript, say page 2. The third part relates to the broad theme that the issue relates to, for example, how children feel travelling to school. So your code now reads T1/P2/T1. You write that in the margin next to the para- graph or section in which that theme is discussed.'

'OK I get it. The code means teacher 1, page 2, and theme 1.'

'Correct. When you have identified all the broad themes in a transcript go a level lower and identify the different issues that make up a single theme. For example, Theme 1 might contain issues to do with a child's fear of traffic, or concerns about meeting children from other schools, older children or worries about strangers.'

'And you would give each of these a code?'

'Precisely. Thus fear of traffic could become T1/P2/TI/I1 or T1/2/1/1. What is essential is that you record, and keep safe, the details of your coding system. Don't think that you will remember it. Write down what each element of the code means. There is nothing worse then coding all your data and then when you return to it a week later you can't remember what some of the codes mean.'

'But couldn't you identify all the issues first and then summarise them into themes?'

'Indeed you could. Personally I like to work from the top down; it seems more logical to me, but that's a personal preference. What's essential is that the coding system is meaningful to you.'

'I can see the point of coding themes and issues but why bother with teacher and page?'

'You may want to report that Teacher 1 held particular views or you may want to quote what they said.'

'But why the page number?'

'If you quote what they said you will need to provide a reference, e.g. T1/P2 etc.'

'Does that mean that I have to provide a copy of the transcript if I quote them?'

'No. Just include a blank copy of your interview questions. But what you must do is keep the transcripts until after the work has been marked just in case your supervisor or marker asks to see where the quote came from.'

'Because they think I might have made it up?'

'You do have a suspicious mind don't you,' he said smiling. 'After you have analysed all four transcripts you take a pair of scissors and cut out each reference and the statement that goes with it. You can then sort the slips of paper that you have into a series of bundles analysed by theme.'

'Right.' I said, anticipating what Richard was about to say. 'What I'll have is the comments of all four teachers on, say, safety and travelling to school in a single bundle and because of the code I will know which teacher said what.'

'Yes, so you can then split the bundles into issues and if only one teacher raised a particular issue you may decide that it is not worth writing about it in your final report. But be careful, sometimes the most interesting and novel ideas are only raised by one person!'

'What you are suggesting is really only a manual cut and paste, isn't it?'

'Absolutely! But you can do the same with a word-processed transcript by using "Comments" to add codes and different colours of highlighter to identify particular themes. That way you can cut and paste from your transcript the same colour of highlight and group comments on related themes together. Qualitative analysis packages work in a similar fashion. You identify issues, code them and then link files with the same codes together for future use. If you have a lot of data to analyse, a package is ideal, but for a small-scale piece of research the manual or computer-based methods I've described are fine.'

'You mentioned using direct quotes from participants, is that normal practice?'

'I think that it's good practice. If you can provide a quote from an interviewee it often brings the issue to life. It grounds the discussion in reality. I'm a big fan of using actual quotes or describing actual events that you have observed but you must ensure that ...'

'You protect the anonymity of the participant at all times,' I finished the sentence for him.

'You read my mind!'

Sam's reflection

14 December

Well so much for coding. I'd been dreading it but from what Richard said it should be fairly straightforward. What I need to do is design a simple coding system that will allow me to trace back where I got the data from and describe the main themes and sub-issues contained within each theme. Sounds easy, we will see.

I quite like the idea of cutting and pasting my data on the computer. This would be very useful for direct quotes as I could just copy & paste

➡

straight from the transcript. I think Richard's a bit of a dinosaur when it comes to using IT. I can see lots of possibilities there. I could use 'bookmarks' for example to mark sections of text that are particularly important. This would be good for quotes too. But there are probably some advantages to using the manual approach. There might be less chance of getting confused and missing an important piece of data.

I was dubious about using quotes from the data I collect. Probably because of what Richard said about not using long quotes in the literature review. But of course a quote from my data isn't copying, it's reporting exactly what I found. Hang on, I've just had a ping moment. If my code identifies the participant I will be able to see how many times I have used a quote from a particular person. That way I will know if I am relying too heavily on the views of one or two people and ignoring others.

Review of tutorial

'So when should I start to analyse my data?'

'That's a good question. Most commentators would say that you should start as soon as possible. But I would urge caution. When you complete an interview or observation or get a questionnaire back, do a quick and dirty interim analysis. But don't spend too much time on it.'

'Why not?'

'Human beings have been described as pattern seeking animals. If you conduct a really detailed analysis on the first document that you receive back you run the risk of identifying certain themes and issues which you then actively look for in later documents and in the process ignore new themes and issues. Effectively what you may have done, with premature analysis, is close your mind to other possibilities.'

'So let me see if I've got this right. What you are suggesting is that I do a quick analysis and then when I have all the data in I should sit down and do a fuller analysis.'

'Effectively yes. That way you have a good idea of the issues that are arising and you will be able to see if you are collecting the sort of data you need to answer your research questions . . .'

'And do something about it if I'm not. While at the same time I avoid the risk of closing my mind to new information.'

'Correct. If you adopt this approach you will reduce the risk of failing to spot interesting data because you are thinking along previously embedded tramlines or because you are dealing with the data in a routine manner. Like a detective seeking an elusive clue you want to be thinking about the data, consciously and subconsciously, over a period of time. Play with the data, take it apart and put it together again. Look for similarities and differences, issues that support or contradict each other and even odd ideas that don't seem to fit. When you have done this you will have started to explore, explain and interpret your data.'

'If I'm going to do that I can't do it in a single sitting can I?'

'Correct. What you are involved in is a process of constant comparison. This is where you constantly review your data and the interpretations you place on them. To do this you need to give yourself adequate time to think about and reflect upon the data you have collected. You might even go and do a little more reading. There really is no single correct way to analyse data you need to find an approach that is right for you and your data. But the cardinal rule has to be "don't rush it".'

Sam's reflection

16 December

I can't believe that it is only nine days to Christmas. I need to get organised. I'm determined to get some useful work done on my project over the holidays as well as having a good time. I need a timetable. And then I need to stick to it.

The two stage process that Richard suggested for analysing data seems sound. I'm constantly amazed at how people's first impressions determine what they think about a person, place or thing. Once they've formed an impression it's really hard to get them to change it. So I can see how dangerous it might to spend too long analysing the first interview schedule or questionnaire.

I'll look at the data as it comes in but I'll also set aside a full week for the final full-blooded analysis. I'll complete the analysis in three sessions but spread them out over the full week. That should give me time to reflect upon the data and try to identify any possible alternative interpretations.

Review of tutorial

'OK now we need to look at questionnaires and observations ...'

For some reason I decided to pre-empt what Richard had to say. Maybe it was because I was starting to feel confident about research theory or because I understood how his mind worked. 'Let me have a go,' I said surprising myself. 'From what you said about interviews, observations and questionnaires all residing on a single continuum between unstructured and structured, I reckon that a similar relationship must exist when it comes to looking at analysis of data.'

'Go on,' he said leaning forward with interest.

'OK,' I said taking a deep breath. 'Let's start with questionnaires. If I have a structured questionnaire, then by default I must have identified in advance the issues that were of interest to me and framed one or more questions about each issue. And if my questionnaire is logically structured, then I will have grouped together questions that explore the same or similar issues. Effectively these groupings will be my themes. Therefore I have my issues and themes already.'

'Very good. But what if it's a semi-structured or unstructured questionnaire?'

I was on a roll and replied confidently, 'In the case of an unstructured questionnaire, I'd treat the responses received like the transcript of an interview. I'd high-light and code the issues pretty much as you outlined earlier.'

'And the semi-structured questionnaire?'

'The semi-structured questionnaire would have some structured questions and some unstructured answers written by the participant. So I'd use a combination of the above approaches. Summarising the responses to the structured questions as outlined previously and treating the participants' comments as a series of excerpts from an interview transcript.'

'Excellent. That is exactly the approach that I would adopt. But what about observation schedules?'

'The same principles apply. The only difference is that where you have a semi-structured observation or an unstructured observations the notes and comments that you will be analysing will be your own rather than the views of the respondent.'

'And what about notes that you have made as a result of participant observations?'

'I'd analysis them just the same as I would an interview transcript.' I paused, a thought floating just outside my consciousness.

'What is it?' asked Richard.

'I was thinking,' I said uncertainly, 'that maybe observation notes are a bit like the notes you take in an interview when you can't record the session, while a reflective diary is more like a full interview transcript. Does that make sense?'

'It does indeed. I wouldn't say that it is a perfect match but it's not a bad analogy. Anything that helps you make sense of what you're doing is useful.'

Sam's reflection

16 December

Heck that felt good. I sounded really confident about what I was saying. Perhaps it is as Richard keeps saying research is a simple process provided you can cut through the jargon and detail and look at the fundamental principles that underpin it. Once you clearly understand them it's possible to think your way through a project. It really isn't rocket science. Which reminds me. Last week when I used that expression one of the kids asked me what phrase do rocket scientists use? There's always one.

Review of tutorial

'So have you got any advice on how best to present the data in the final report?'

'Some. As we have previously discussed what you need to do in the findings is analyse the data that you have collected. Because qualitative data is mainly concerned with words it's usually presented in a discursive manner. Typically you would report or describe the data and then analyse it using the theories in your literature review to explain, explore and challenge what you have found. You can then use your own powers of logic, induction and deduction to dig into the data, while all the time looking for alternative interpretations.'

'But what about diagrams and tables?'

'I was coming to that. There is no reason why you can't use many of the tools that quantitative researchers use to present their data such as bar charts, histograms and pie charts. We will be looking at these in the next tutorial on quantitative data analysis and there are some simple examples on my website (**www.pearsoned.co.uk/colesmcgrath**) on how they can be applied in qualitative research. But for the moment I'd just like to look at how you can use tables to summarise qualitative data.'

'Do you want me to look at the examples on the website before our next meeting?'

'That would be very helpful. But for the moment let's stick with tables. You will need to refer to my handout for today as we go through this. (*See handout.*)

'Suppose you undertake four semi-structured interviews and you want to summarise, compare and contrast the views of the participants. You could produce a table where each participant is given a column and the interview questions are listed down the side. You could also do this with the themes you've identified from your initial analysis. It is then possible to enter for each person or theme a quote and summary of the responses. This both summarises, compares and contrasts the responses of the participants using very few words. You can then analyse and comment on the table to your heart's content.'

'Could I use the same approach to summarise the theories or definitions of different writers in my literature review?'

'Absolutely. As I always say, anything that helps you to communicate more clearly with your reader is to be welcomed. Tables are also really useful for summarising data from questionnaires, though a bar chart can be really useful for presenting data from Likert-type questions. Either way it's vital that your presentation is consistent. For example, when describing your results you wouldn't report that 60 per cent of people disagreed or disagreed strongly with Statement 1 while 80 per cent agreed or agreed strongly with Statement 2. Instead you would say either: 60 per cent of people disagreed or disagreed strongly with Statement 1 and 20 per cent disagreed or disagreed strongly with statement 2, or that 40 per cent of people agreed or agreed strongly with Statement 1 and 80 per cent agreed or agreed strongly with Statement 2. Can you see that I am being consistent in how I present the data?'

'I understand the consistency angle but why use percentages, wouldn't it be easier for people to understand if you used actual figures such as 9 out of 10 people agreed or agreed strongly?'

'You might think so. But what if you have 10 questionnaires returned and only 7 people have answered all the questions. That means that some questions may have as few as 7 responses. People would find it difficult to compare 8 out of 10 people agreed or agreed strongly with Statement 1 while 6 out of 7 agreed or agreed strongly with Statement 2. Shown as percentages the figures would become 80 per cent compared to 86 per cent.'

'So again it is about clarity and consistency.'

'Precisely. The last method of presentation that I'd like to cover is the use of pictures and diagrams. It's true what they say that one picture can be worth a thousand words. So think about how you might use pictures to represent your findings.'

'I'm not sure that my data will lend itself to such an approach.'

'Don't be so sure. Sometimes a picture can capture what people feel better than words. This is just off the top of my head, but you could think about drawing a picture of a school and surrounding area and by using different colours show which areas children find most frightening. So, for example, if they are frightened of travelling to and from school the roads could be coloured in dark blue or black and if they felt safest in school perhaps the classrooms would be yellow. I'm not saying that this tells you a great deal but it gives you an immediate and very striking impression of the findings.'

'I've not seen that approach used in journals.'

'Maybe not but give it time. It was only a few years ago that academia disparaged the use of story telling as a form of research. But times are changing.'

'And diagrams?'

'These are common. Just look at any textbook. They are often used to encapsulate a theory or idea and they are a great way to summarise a lot of information using very few words. The thing to do is be creative. To think about your data in terms of three-dimensional models not just two-dimensional words on a page. But – and this is important – you still have to explain and analyse your data. The picture or diagram by itself is not enough.'

Sam's reflection

18 December

I'm quite excited about using pictures and diagrams to represent my data. It'll give me a chance to be creative and try something different. But I need to keep it sensible I don't want to do a Tracey Emin or

Damien Hirst on my data. The pictures have to be more than artistic and eye-catching, they have to serve a purpose, which is to make my findings clearer to the reader.

Right that's me finished until 27 December – time to relax and enjoy life.

Record of tutorial

Student: Sam Sylon   **Date: 13/12/XX**
SUMMARY OF KEY LEARNING POINTS

- Whether you use a computer package or a pen and paper you will have to devise a coding system.

- The coding system should enable you to trace where a piece of data came from and analyse it to at last two levels, e.g. theme and issue. It is essential that you keep a record of your coding system and that you update it as the system develops and expands.

- It is not normally necessary to include completed copies of your data collection tool as an appendix, a blank copy will usually suffice. However, you should keep all material (tapes, transcripts, observation schedules, completed questionnaires) until after your work has been marked. They should then be destroyed.

- Once the data have been coded, sort the material by theme and issue. This can be done manually using a hard copy or by computer using cut and paste. The process for both is essentially the same.

- In addition to reporting your findings, use selected extracts from your data to bring your study to life, e.g. actual quotes from interviews or questionnaires.

- Analysis of data should never become a mechanical task. Carry out a 'quick and dirty' analysis soon after collection of the data but leave the main analysis until you have completed your data collection. ➡

- Undertake the final analysis of data over a period of time and definitely not at one marathon session. Give yourself time to think and reflect on the data. Write notes on what you have found and constantly refer back to your literature.

- A well designed questionnaire will have sections that could be described as themes and individual questions that relate to specific issues. Where a participant has been asked to add a comment to a question these can be treated as notes from an interview for the purpose of analysis.

- A well designed structured observation schedule will have sections that could be described as themes and individual headings that relate to specific issues. Where a semi-structured or unstructured approach has been adopted, the observation notes may be treated as notes from an interview for the purpose of analysis.

- Qualitative data are normally presented in a discursive format. The researcher reports the findings before analysing the data using the ideas and theories contained in their literature review and their own understanding of the issues and powers of deduction and induction.

- You should also seek to add impact to your presentation by considering the use of tables, diagrams and pictures.

Agreed action points

Sam will:

- Produce a short document describing how and when the analysis of data will be undertaken.

- Design a simple data coding system.

- Consider to what extent tables, diagrams and pictures might be used in the final report to enhance clarity and understanding of the findings.

Analysis of qualitative data

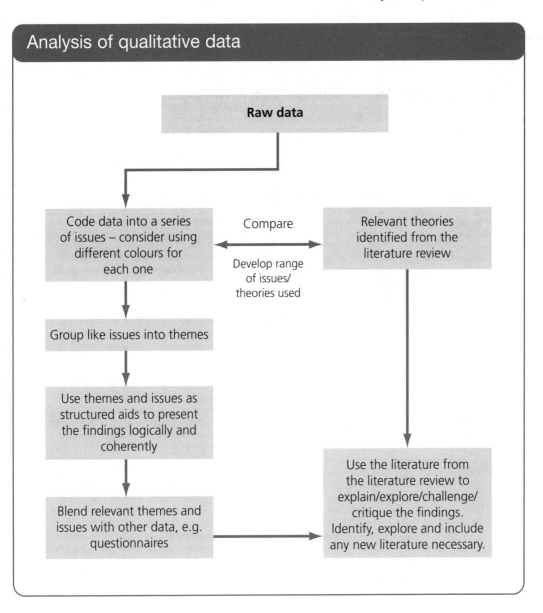

Handout

USE OF TABLES TO SUMMARISE AND PRESENT QUALITATIVE DATA

Table 1 – Summarising selected quotes from interview schedule

Question	Teacher 1	Teacher 2	Head of year	Head-teacher
How would you describe the style of management within the school?	At times I think it is quite relaxed but at inspection it can be very controlling.	I think that by and large it is very autocratic. Only the views of certain people are taken into account.	I find that it is a nice balance between task and concern for the person. Much better than my last school.	I like to think that we are a team and that there are no real chiefs just a lot of hard-working professionals who each contribute at the appropriate time.
Where do you think the power lies in the school?	With the senior management team.	With the head, what she says goes.	With the head and senior management team but they do listen to the staff.	In the main with the staff. We seldom do anything without asking for their views first. Of course sometimes SMT has to take unpopular decisions.

Table 2 – Summarising responses to Likert Questionnaire

Response to the question, I think that:	% that agree or agree strongly with the statement
Senior management team take the views of staff into account when making their decisions.	60
The head-teacher is able to impose her views on the senior management team.	50
The head-teacher is able to impose her views on the governors.	80
The head-teacher is approachable and willing to listen to my views.	70

Table 3 – Summary of 'impressions' gained from participants on key issues by position in hierarchy

Position	Concern for task	Concern for person	Trust in staff	Level of control exercised over staff
Head	High	High	High	Medium
SMT member	High	Medium	High	Medium
Head of year	High	Medium/low	Low	High
Teacher	High	Low	Low/very low	Very high

Note: Table 3 is an example of how you might summarise qualitative data in order to give the reader an impression or overview of your findings. In this case it appears that the further down the hierarchy teachers are, the more likely they are to think that management is more concerned with 'getting the job done' than the well-being of staff.

Diagram

Key to diagram:

Controlled = Staff who are trusted because they do not rock the boat but they are not necessarily respected by management.

Colleague = Staff who are both respected and trusted by the management because their views and beliefs coincide with those of SMT.

Conspirator = Staff who are respected for their experience or academic standing but not trusted because they have a different ideology or vision for education to that of management.

Combatant = Staff who are at war with school management, sometimes for personal reasons, who are neither respected nor trusted.

Diagram 1 – How staff perceive their relationship with management

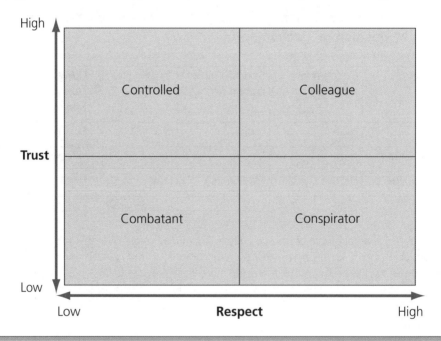

Additional information on the issues covered by this tutorial can be found at/in:

- www.pearsoned.co.uk/colesmcgrath
- Denscombe, M. (2008) *The Good Research Guide (3rd ed.).* McGraw Hill: Maidenhead, Ch.14.
- Cohen, L., Mannion, L. and Morrison, K. (2007) *Research Methods in Education (6th ed.).* Routledge Falmer: London, Ch.22.
- Newby, P. (2010) *Research Methods for Education.* Longman, Pearson: Harlow, Ch. 11.

ANALYSIS OF QUANTITATIVE DATA

Aim of tutorial

To enable you to analyse, evaluate and report quantitative data. A range of approaches to analysing and presenting quantitative data are presented and explained. It is suggested that you skim-read this tutorial and then study the examples given at the end of the tutorial and on the website **www.pearsoned.co.uk/colesmcgrath** before reading the tutorial again more carefully.

Contents

→ Primary and secondary data

→ Continuous and discontinuous data

→ Range, mean, mode and median

→ Descriptive statistics

→ Variables

→ Hypotheses

→ Presenting data

→ Spread and standard deviation

→ Probability

→ Comparing means

→ Analysing a Likert response

2 January

A new year and what am I thinking about? New Year's resolutions, holidays, what major changes the year will bring for me? No, I'm thinking I need to send Richard some examples of data for the next session as we're going to talk about quantitative methods. For some reason he's asked me to send him some test score data although it has nothing to do with my research. I bet he will tell me it's about using a wide range of research tools. At this stage of the course I'd be happy just to use the ones I need to pass the assignment!

I remember that there's a continuum between quantitative and qualitative analysis, so I must ask about my data and check my understanding about where it comes on that scale. Since much of it's based on people's opinions I need to be careful not to make claims I can't support. I'm particularly interested in how to present my data in an understandable format. So often I see charts that I don't understand and the message just isn't clear. I'll send some data from my questionnaires and observations a few days before the session. I also have some figures from a government department website that I could do with analysing.

Review of tutorial

'Thanks for the data Sam; it really does help to have something before the session. It means I can have a good look at it beforehand.'

'I hope you're impressed; I actually remembered this time!'

'It wouldn't have anything to do with the fact that this session is about quantitative analysis would it?'

'Well, now you mention it . . .'

'Can you remember what I said about the first step in data analysis?'

'You said that it begins with the design of the data-gathering instruments. I remember that you often get asked to analyse data and that it's difficult to do a good job when this hasn't been considered at the planning stage.'

'Absolutely. It's like designing a car without any idea of how it will be used.'

'And by the time the customer gets it it's too late.'

'True, though it's not quite as disastrous as that. Can you remember how you would deal with this potential problem?'

'I thought beforehand about the value of being able to make quantitative statements about my data when it's based on attitudes and opinions. Where I thought that it would be useful to gauge the strength of opinion I included a Likert scale to give me some opportunity to make some semi-quantitative statements. I felt that this was important. I suppose that if I'd been using observations I could have included a timeline and a tally of different events by males and females for example?'

'Good thinking. With the Likert you've provided yourself with the opportunity to include an element of quantitative analysis. You're absolutely right that care is needed when interpreting these types of data. For example, if you collect some **demographic** data on a group, maybe on gender or ethnicity, you can express the different groups as a percentage and be very sure that the number you have is representative of your sample and therefore you can make confident statements about the data.'

'Because I counted each one and therefore the data will be accurate.'

'True. Though in the case of numbers based on attitudes and opinions you can't be quite so sure. This doesn't mean that it's not worth making quantitative statements, but it does mean that you need to exercise caution when making deductions about them. Like castles built on sand really.'

Sam's reflection

10 January

Why on earth bother with quantitative analysis when there are limits to what I can do with the findings? I suppose that's just my way of trying to avoid it. I liked the 'castles built on sand' analogy. There are some things that I can measure and be sure of, like the ethnicity of the pupils in my class, but people's attitudes and opinions are like the sand; they shift all the time. So I might make some quantitative statements, but they would depend on the participants' perceptions of my questions and only hold for those people at one point in time and they wouldn't be generalisable.

Review of tutorial

'Let's talk about types of data now and then we'll talk about probability. There are a few important terms here, namely primary and secondary data and continuous and discontinuous data.'

'I've heard of primary and secondary. Primary is raw data like the number of boys or girls in a class and secondary is when something has been done to the primary data such as calculating the percentage of boys and girls. I'm not sure about continuous and discontinuous though.'

'You're right about primary and secondary data. Continuous data is data that can be represented on a number scale, such as your height. Discontinuous doesn't usually involve numbers, but categories like male or female. For example, consider ethnicity, the duration of a lesson, test scores and GCSE grades. Which could be classed as continuous and which discontinuous?'

'Duration of a lesson is continuous. They seem to go on for ever sometimes! So are test scores. Grades are continuous because they go in sequence; A, B, C, etc. and ethnicity is discontinuous.'

'Nearly right. GCSE scores are effectively discontinuous because the grades produce separate categories which students fall into rather than numbers. Of course when I took them they were numbered grades!'

'I suppose you had to use a quill as well?' I said smiling. Richard screwed his nose up, but before he could respond I said, 'But surely they were also categories because you only had the option of Grade 1, 2, etc?'

'Good point! This is a debatable one. Of course if you take an average numerical score of all the children in a class, then it's continuous because you wouldn't necessarily end up with whole numbers.'

'Let's leave that one there! What's next?'

'It's worth mentioning **descriptive** or **summary statistics**.'

'Not statistics already?'

'These are very straightforward statistics. The word statistics just means "figures", "data", or "information". It doesn't necessarily mean complex calculations. Descriptive or summary statistics just means basic manipulation of primary data to produce percentages or means, for example. In many cases it's sufficient to stop there.'

'So maybe I could get away with descriptive stats for my data?' I said hopefully.

'Possibly, but I'd like you to have a go at one or two more methods. You don' t need a detailed understanding of the maths. Just use statistical methods as a tool. Excel will do everything that you need. For example, if you have a series of test scores just put them into Excel and follow the path: Tools>Analysis>Descriptive statistics. Select "Summary statistics". Then select the column or row of numbers and click "OK". You'll get various summary stats such as **mean**, **standard deviation**, **range**, sum, **modal** and **median**. Have a look at the website for more details of this.'

'I remember those terms. But I get them confused, especially the mean and median. Can you just remind me what they mean?'

'Well the range is straightforward. It's the spread between the highest and lowest number. To calculate it you just subtract the lowest figure from the highest.'

'That simple?'

'I told you stats were easy. The mean is the total of all the scores added together divided by the number of scores.'

'OK. So what's the median and modal?'

'The median is the middle score. To work it out you list every single score in order – even if the same number is repeated several times – then look for the middle one. If there's an even number of scores, then the median is between the numbers either side of the middle two scores. The modal is just the most common score. There's an example on this handout.'

Sam's reflection

10 January

I imagine that the range would be useful to give me an idea of the spread of my data, to see if there are large differences between the bottom and the top. This might be useful when analysing responses to a Likert-type question to see if opinions are quite similar or very varied. I could compare mean scores to look at the difference between two groups such as males and females. The modal score would tell me the most common number of questions they got right and the median is the middle score. I'm still not clear how these would be used though.

Review of tutorial

'Can you just clarify why it could be useful to quote a median, rather than a mean?'

'Supposing you had a lot of high scores and a few very low ones. The mean would just tell you the average score, rather than giving an idea of how these were distributed. The middle, or modal score would be a better indicator of whether they were skewed to one extreme or the other. Have a look at the website for an example of this in practice ... Now we need to talk about **hypotheses** and variables.'

'Do we have to?'

'Yes. These are two terms that are at the heart of quantitative analysis. We talked about the nature of quantitative data in Tutorial 4 and I mentioned that hypotheses were a feature of this approach. Remember that they're predictions based on a theory. Hypotheses predict how one variable might change when another changes and it's an important aspect of this approach that only one variable is changed at a time and the others are controlled.'

'I remember that there are two types of variable. One you change and the other you measure.'

'Good. The **independent variable** is the one you change and the **dependent** one is the one you measure. It's important to bear these two types of variables in mind when you present data because there are conventions to consider.'

'So, for example, test questions are the independent variable and the scores are the dependent one. My hypothesis could be to predict how test scores would change if I included different questions?' I said.

'It certainly could. That brings us to the presentation of data. Tables are an important way of summarising data, but it's difficult to interpret trends from them. Graphs and charts show these trends better, but there are conventions for their use. Charts are usually in the form of bars or columns and they tend to be used for discontinuous data like recording the achievement of different ethnic groups, whereas graphs show continuous data. The convention is that the independent variable goes on the horizontal axis and the dependent one on the vertical axis.'

'So ethnicity would go on the horizontal and the test score on the vertical in the case of the bar chart.'

'Yes, though it's really a column chart if the bars are vertical. It's also worth remembering that the columns are separate too as there's no continuous relationship between the different ethnic groups. They're separate entities.'

'But I've seen charts with the columns together. What's the difference?'

'These are **histograms**, essentially frequency distributions. An example would be plotting the height of pupils in a class. Height is continuous, but it can be represented as categories. For example, 1.4 to 1.5 metres. You would plot the number of pupils in each category and the result would be a bell-shaped graph or distribution. This is usually called a **normal distribution**, though technically the sort of result you get is likely to approximate to a normal distribution as there may be slightly more short pupils than tall ones, so the graph wouldn't be symmetrical.

We'll come back to this later. How do you think that you would show continuous data?'

'Maybe as a line graph?'

'Usually, yes. In this case you're justified in joining the points because you can often assume a continuous relationship between them. For example, you might record test scores for a pupil at different times and plot his or her score over time. Potentially this enables you to predict intermediate scores, or extrapolate into the future to predict possible future scores. Line graphs can also be used to probe relationships between different variables. This is called a **scatterplot**.'

'How would I use one of those?'

'Supposing you wanted to compare punctuality with distance between the school and home. You would assume that punctuality increases as distance decreases, but you don't know this.'

'So I could record punctuality and look at records to find the distance.'

'You would plot those on separate axes and look at the correlation – in other words the way in which one variable moves in relation to the other – between them. You may then be able to state whether there's no correlation, a positive correlation – punctuality increases with distance – or a negative correlation in which punctuality decreases with distance. Have a look at this handout for examples of these (*see below*). Finally, how could you represent percentages, of say religious groups in a class?'

'I suppose I could use a bar chart with a bar for each group.'

'Well you could, but there's an alternative. Here's a clue. You would be able to show the proportion of a whole.'

'Oh you mean a **pie chart**.'

'Correct. Of course you can get Excel to do all these charts and figures for you. The danger is that you're shown a bewildering number of options. The key is to ensure that you stick to the basic rules relating to axis that we've already discussed and that clarity is the guiding principle. It's too easy to choose a format that's the most attractive when it actually makes the data more difficult to understand.'

Sam's reflection

12 January

So although there are some rules about variables, axis and types of graph or chart, the key is clarity. The point of presenting data is to make it easier to interpret and I mustn't let design get in the way of function. Plotting data can also enable me to get more out of it, for instance by being able to predict trends in the future by extrapolating. I can see that this is useful for my data, but I could also take data from reports, websites and journals for example and perhaps choose to present all or part of it in a different way to support or challenge the argument that I'm making.

Review of tutorial

'It's also vital that you comment on data presented in figures, charts and graphs in your text. Don't just assume that the reader understands why it's there, what it shows, or what it means. Take them by the hand and explain the data's purpose, relevance and importance.'

'I remember that each chart needs a title and a number.'

'A title certainly, but there's also the legend. The title concisely summarises what the chart shows and it's usually placed at the top, but the legend includes a sentence or two of explanation and it goes underneath with the figure number. Tables are called 'Table 1' and so on and everything else, including charts and diagrams, is called a figure. In a longer assignment with chapters you can use the chapter number first, so 1.1 would mean Chapter 1 Figure 1 and so on.'

'I'm starting to get worried,' I said.

'Why for heaven's sake?'

'So far it's been OK. But I feel that it should be more complicated than you've described, after all none of this can actually help me to prove anything.'

'Hang on. Remember what I said at the beginning that you're not really looking to prove anything. You're building a picture of a set of circumstances and how they affect human behaviour. It's a great aspiration to want to prove something, but in reality we produce observations which may be relatable to other circumstances. Communication is really important and good academic writing is about clarifying complex ideas; putting them in a simple way. Certainly statistics are helpful but they must be used cautiously and only when they can add to the discussion, particularly when qualitative or semi-qualitative methods are used. The other point is that even when you do use statistics, they don't enable you to prove anything. They just give you a **probability** that what you observe is due to chance and you still have to make a judgement about how significant this is.'

'I can't believe that I am going to say this but, and it's a big but, if I were undertaking quantitative research what sorts of other things could Excel do with my data?'

'Well the first thing you could consider is to get an idea of the spread of your data by calculating the standard deviation of your mean. So let's go back to your test score data. You could get a mean score of say 55 per cent as a result of a set of test scores which ranged either between 40 and 60 per cent or 30 and 70 per cent for example and you wouldn't know what the spread was just from the mean. Of course you can see this by looking at the scores, but it helps to be able to put a number on how spread out the scores are. You can do this in Excel. Just select STDEV from the Insert menu, select your data and click OK. Versions of Excel differ, but the principle will be the same. You can then quote your mean to plus or minus the standard deviation. So if your standard deviation of the 55 per cent score was 10 per cent, you could say the mean score was 55 per cent plus or minus 10 per cent. The larger value for the standard deviation, the more spread out your data are.'

'Fine, so why is spread important?'

'Well, in the case of test scores you actually want them to be spread out so that the test is discriminating between different levels of achievement towards your learning objectives, so the standard deviation can be helpful here. It can be important to know how variable your data are. Let's say you're measuring percentage attendance every month and you calculate a mean. It helps to know how much it varies over that period. The standard deviation can also help you with graphs where you're plotting means. You can plot each point and then plot plus and minus one standard deviation above and below; this is called an error bar. These can help you to draw a line of best fit through the data. There's an example of a standard deviation calculation on my website (**www.pearsoned.co.uk/colesmcgrath**).'

Sam's reflection

12 January

I remember the bell-shaped graph. I thought that I would have to plot one of these every time I want to measure spread, but I've realised that I needn't do this. All I have to do is put the data in and do a standard deviation with Excel. And I can quote the spread around my mean. Maybe this would be useful for attendance data too. I could compare the variability between different classes.

Review of tutorial

'You mentioned probability earlier. What is it and why is it important?'

'We deal in probability all the time. Some things have a high probability and others a low probability.'

'Like winning the Lottery!'

'Yes, a very low probability. But how is probability measured?'

'I know that there's a one in two chance of a coin showing heads or tails.'

'Except on those rare occasions when it lands on its side. So yes, that's one way, but you could also express the same probability of one in two as a percentage or a decimal.'

'So that would be 50 per cent or point five?'

'Absolutely. So probability is the likelihood of something happening. Another important word is **significance**. What do you think this means?'

'A result is significant if it's important in terms of the research question.'

'It is, yes, but there's a more technical definition involving probability. A difference between two means – for example, the test scores of boys and the test scores of girls – is said to be significant if there's a less than 5 per cent likelihood of it being due to chance alone. Many statistical tests give you a figure for probability. This tells you what the likelihood is of the difference between two means being due purely to chance; in other words resulting from the random fluctuation of events.'

'So if there's a low probability – say 5 per cent – of it being due to chance, then there's a high probability that it's not due to chance and that the difference is real!' I said.

'Yes, a 95 per cent probability. I'm not sure about the "real" bit though, but certainly some other factor than just chance has produced the difference.'

'Why does it always seem to be 95 per cent?'

'How sure do you need to be? If you were 95 per cent sure that you would win the lottery, wouldn't that be enough? So if you're 95 per cent sure – or there's a 95 per cent probability – that a difference between two means is not just due to chance, then maybe you can make valid statements about the data. In practice, you look at the value for the probability and make a judgement. For example, in drug trials being 95 per cent sure that a drug is safe isn't enough.'

'I'd want to be 100 per cent sure!'

'Well, that's almost impossible to achieve, but maybe 99.9999 etcetera. When we use statistical tests, we're testing our hypothesis. It's worth mentioning here that there are two types of hypotheses. When making predictions, we may predict that one variable has an effect on the other, or that it does not have an effect. For example that gender either does or does not have an effect on test scores. The former is called an **alternate hypothesis** and the latter a **null hypothesis**. Statistical tests are used to arrive at the probability of a hypothesis being correct and we usually use them to test the null hypothesis.'

'Why's the null hypothesis used for statistical tests, rather than the alternate one? I might think that one variable does have an effect on another, yet I have to say that it doesn't!'

'It's just convention. Either way, the value for probability helps you to confirm or refute whichever hypothesis you choose by giving you a probability that the result is due to chance ...'

'So give me an example of a test that I could use.'

'The **Student's t-test** is a good one for comparing means.'

'An appropriate name!'

'Indeed. The test was developed by William Sealy Gosset for the Guinness company in the early 1900s. "Student" was his pen name.'

'Is this where the null hypothesis comes in?'

'It is. So what would it be if we're comparing boys' and girls' test scores?

'That there's no significant difference between them?'

'Yes. So we either confirm that null hypothesis if the test shows that there's a greater than 5 per cent probability that the difference between the scores is due to chance alone or refute it if there's less than 5 per cent chance.'

'So how do I calculate it?'

'Our old friend Excel again. Enter your data – say the scores for boys and girls – into two separate columns. Click on an empty cell and insert the t-test function from the Insert menu. Select each column of data in turn in the "array" boxes. Generally choose "two tailed" in the next box and "unequal variance" in the final box. Click "OK" and the probability appears in the cell.'

'Seems straightforward.'

'It is, and there's an example on the website. But as I said, it's what you do with the result that's important. The probability value you get is the probability that the difference you see is due to chance, so the lower the value, the more likely that the scores are really different.'

'And usually I'm looking for a value less than point zero five.'

'Yes, though remember that you can change that number according to how sure you want to be.'

Sam's reflection

13 January

I can't see me using the t-test a lot, but it could be useful for looking at school evaluation data. I could compare different schools' data on such things as achievement and attendance. I could also take data from government reports and make comparisons there too. These are examples of where I could make more valid statements as these are empirical data not based on attitudes and opinions. I thought that this 95 per cent probability was fixed for some reason, but I like the idea of being able to make up my own mind. Even a 60 or 70 per cent probability could sometimes be enough.

So I suppose that I could gather some attendance data. And compare the attendance of children who are concerned with their safety with that of those who aren't according to the questionnaire results. My null hypothesis would be that there's no difference between the attendance of the two groups. If my t-test result gives a probability of less than 5 per cent, then I can reject my null hypothesis and state that there is a difference between the groups. Eureka, I've got it!

Review of tutorial

'As you know I'm going to use Likert-style questions in my questionnaire. You said previously that they are a good example of a semi-quantitative approach. So how would I analyse those results?'

'There are several ways. Because Likert scales are always a response to a statement in terms of agreement or disagreement you can give each response a number. So "Strongly agree" would be 5 and agree 4 and so on.'

'That would allow me to summarise the strength of opinion for or against a particular statement.'

'Correct. The simplest comparison is to score the number of respondents giving a particular response to a statement. This could then be quoted as a percentage and maybe plotted as a column chart with one column for each response. The pattern for different questions could easily be compared. You could also multiply the number of respondents for each response by the number allocated to it. For example, if you had seven respondents indicating strong agreement, and you had allocated 5 to this category as you suggest, then you would multiply 7 by 5 to give a score of 35.'

'Then if I added up the scores for each category, that would give me a measure of agreement as the stronger the agreement, the higher the score.'

'So how would you show that?'

'I could plot the measure of agreement for each question on a column chart. That would help me compare the questions,' I said.

'Yes. Remember in the last tutorial we talked about organising your questionnaire in such a way that questions to do with the same issues are grouped together under a particular theme. This then allows you to compare the level of agreement within each theme.'

'But we talked about probability and you haven't mentioned anything to do with that on Likert scales.'

'Why do you think that is?'

'Because they're based on attitudes and opinions, so it's dodgy to make quantitative statements.'

'Correct but it's worth a go though. There are still a couple of approaches you can take. We've talked about the t-test, so for a given statement you could record the response for each respondent and calculate a mean by dividing the sum of the scores by the number of participants.'

'And the t-test compares means, so I could compare the mean for pairs of questions, say question one compared with question two and this would give me a probability that they're significantly different . . .'

'Yes you could, but there are other valid tests such as the **Chi squared** which you could use. It's tricky to explain and not commonly used so I've put an example on the website. It could be used to look at a single question to test the probability that the distribution of responses – let's say 10 respondents ticked "strongly disagree", six "agree" and so on – is significantly different from the situation where the number of people indicating each response is the same.'

'If it's the same, then they're not giving a strong opinion either way, so I suppose it could give an idea of how opinionated they are.'

'It could, but we'll leave this session there as we've covered a lot today.'

Sam's reflection

14 January

I'm going to stick to charting Likert results. Maybe the stats are a bridge too far this time. I'll have a look at the example on the website though.

So the message here was that it's always worth having a go at quantitative analysis, but if attitudes and opinions are involved I need to be cautious interpreting the results. I can see the difference now between the qualitative and quantitative approaches. They seem so different that it's difficult to imagine that they're on a continuum. It's much clearer to me now why it's so important to consider how data will be analysed as the research instruments are designed, rather than leaving this until I've collected the data when it's too late.

Record of tutorial

Student: Sam Sylon   **Date: 9/1/XX**

SUMMARY OF KEY LEARNING POINTS

- Plan for the analysis as well as the collection of data. This includes qualitative and quantitative approaches.

- Be cautious when using quantitative methods to make statements based on attitudes and opinions.

- Primary data are raw data. This becomes secondary data when it is manipulated, for example by calculating percentages.

- Continuous data are data represented by a numerical scale such as height. Discontinuous data are categorical such as gender.

- Descriptive or summary statistics involve representing data as means, ranges, modals, medians and percentages, for example.

- Excel or similar spreadsheets can do many straightforward statistical calculations using formats familiar to people with basic IT skills.

- There are two types of variables: independent (the one changed) and dependent (the one measured).

- There are two types of hypotheses: alternate (independent affects dependent variable) and null (independent does not affect the dependent variable).

- Bar charts are used to display discontinuous data unless it's a frequency distribution (histogram) and line graphs are used to display continuous data. Percentages can be displayed using pie charts.

- Everything that is not a table is a figure. Tables and figures need a title and a legend with an identifying number. Always make comments on them in the text.

- Statistics seldom prove anything, they just provide a probability that any difference is not just due to chance.

- Putting a value on the spread of your data can be a useful indicator of variability. Calculating a standard deviation for your mean can achieve this.

- Probability is the likelihood of something happening and it's usually quoted as a decimal or a percentage.   ➡

- Differences between data are said to be significant if there's a less than 5 per cent chance that the differences are due to chance alone. This is convention and can be changed according to how sure you want to be.
- Statistical tests are used to provide a probability in order to confirm or refute the null hypothesis.
- The Student's t-test can be used to provide a probability that two means are significantly different.
- Likert scales can be analysed by plotting percentage responses. You can then calculate a mean strength of opinion and compare questions using the t-test and by using Chi-squared which compares actual and expected responses.

Agreed action points

Sam will:

- Identify opportunities for collecting numerical data relevant to the research questions.
- Plan for the analysis of these data by considering the use of descriptive statistics, standard deviation and the Student's t-test.
- Consider how the data will be presented and select data for appendices and the main body of the report.
- Practise using Excel to produce appropriate graphs and charts.

Analysis and presentation of quantitative data

Data in the form of numbers? — No → Qualitive analytical methods

Yes ↓

Quantitative analytical methods

↓

Design tables for raw data collection

↓

Descriptive statistics – mean, modal, median, range, percentages

↓

Further statistical methods?

No ↓   Yes ↓

Choose data presentation methods   Begin with spread, e.g. standard deviation

↓

Compare means, e.g. t-test. Compare observed with expected, e.g. Chi squared or research further methods

Discontinuous data?	Continuous data?	Percentages?	Frequency distribution?
↓	↓	↓	↓
Bar/column chart	Line graph	Pie chart	Histogram

Handout

DESCRIPTIVE STATISTICS

The simplest statistical test is to calculate a mean or average for a series of numbers such as test scores. Here are some test scores:

Table 1

Pupil	A	B	C	D	E	F	G	H	I	J	K	L	M	N
Score	5	9	12	8	8	6	7	8	7	3	11	2	10	4

- Use Table 1 to calculate the *mean* test result by adding all the scores and dividing by the number of individual scores.
- Determine the *median* or middle test score by ranking them (put them in ascending order).
- Determine the *modal* or most common score.
- Determine the *range* of the scores by subtracting the lowest from the highest.

The answers are:

Answers.
Mean 7.1
Median 7.5
Modal 8.0
Range 10.0

Handout

DATA PRESENTATION

Here are a few different types of display device.

Scattergraph

Used to investigate whether there's a relationship between two variables. The points are not initially joined. For example, the relationship between attendance and distance from home to school:

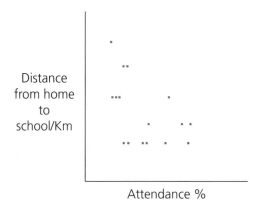

Distance from home to school/Km

Attendance %

Line graph

These are used to display the expected relationship between two variables, when this relationship is continuous, e.g. the mean assessment score of a group over time. The relationship may be:

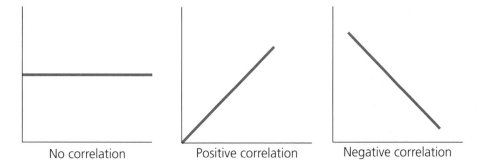

No correlation   Positive correlation   Negative correlation

Column or bar chart (there is a difference!)

These are used when the relationship between variables is discontinuous, e.g. the number of pupils in a class of a particular religion. Note that the bars or columns are separated by a space.

Here's an example of a column chart:

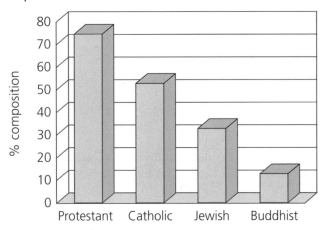

(Adapted from: http://hospiweb.qmuc.ac.uk/imrestxt/quantit/organis.htm)

Histogram

These are designed to show a frequency distribution

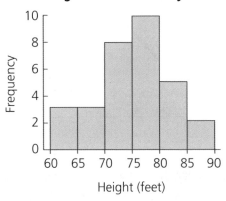

(Obtained from http://en.wikipedia.org/wiki/Histogram)

Pie charts

These are used to display proportions of a whole, usually as percentages:

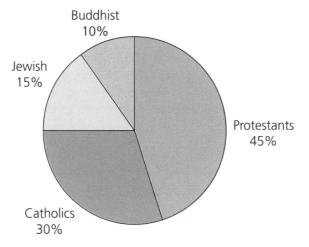

(Adapted from http://hospiweb.qmuc.ac.uk/imrestxt/quantit/organis.htm)

Additional information on the issues covered by this tutorial can be found at/in:

- www.pearsoned.co.uk/colesmcgrath
- Cohen, L., Mannion, L. and Morrison, K. (2007) *Research Methods in Education (6th ed.).* Routledge Falmer: London, Ch.24.
- Denscombe, M. (2008) *The Good Research Guide (3rd ed.).* McGraw Hill: Maidenhead, Ch.13.
- Newby, P. (2010) *Research Methods for Education.* Longman, Pearson: Harlow, Chs.12, 13.

SOME FINAL ADVICE

Aim of tutorial

To help you maximise the mark you achieve by highlighting a number of common errors made by students and suggesting strategies for how to avoid them.

Contents

→ Finding a critical friend

→ Accessing student support

→ The importance of a final edit and polish

→ Demonstrating your understanding and mastery of the theories used

→ One simple trick to improve your literature review

→ Deciding what goes in the appendices

→ How much analysis is enough?

→ Producing work at the required standard

→ What to do with unexpected findings

Sam's reflection

21 January

Today is my final research tutorial. I have to admit that I've enjoyed the sessions more than I thought I would. Mind you I still have the hard bit to do. I have to complete the analysis of the data and write up my findings. Thankfully I'll still be able to contact Richard for advice if I run into difficulties and he will be reading my report as I write it.

Richard said that today's session would be fairly short as he just wanted to highlight ways to improve my final submission and minimise any last minute problems. He also wants to give me the opportunity to ask any questions that I might have. So I had better have a think before the session.

Review of tutorial

When I entered the office Richard was gazing into the distance with that semi-bereaved look that football fans get when it becomes clear that their team is likely to be relegated. What is it about football that can a make reasonably intelligent man act like a child whose favourite toy has just been broken? Thinking that it was probably best not to mention Albion's latest mauling I handed him the cup of coffee that I had picked up for him in the Café Metropolis.

He must have guessed what I was thinking because as he took the coffee he smiled.

'I didn't say a thing,' I said, and sat down.

'But you were thinking it! OK let's get down to it. For our final session I just want to give you some pointers on how you might improve your final submission and also provide you with an opportunity to raise any questions that you might have.'

'OK. But didn't we discuss writing the research report in Tutorial 2?'

'Indeed we did. And now would be a good time to revisit your notes for Tutorial 2. The advice on how to structure your assignment will mean a lot more to you now that you have completed the course. However, I want to emphasise a couple of issues and raise some new points. Everything I'm going to say is based on the comments that markers and external examiners have made to me over the years. What's interesting is that the same comments are made year after year.'

Richard's final comment was delivered in the sort of voice that said 'but you won't make these mistakes will you?' I picked up my pen and waited to be enlightened.

Richard gave me a copy of a handout and said, 'This contains advice on the common errors to avoid when writing your project and some suggestions on how to improve your work with minimum effort. I'm not going to go through them all. Rather I'll emphasise the ones that can improve your marks the most.'

I liked the sound of that.

'Firstly you need to find a critical friend to read your work prior to submission.'

'But won't you, as my supervisor, be reading the report?'

'I will read and comment on each section. Part of my feedback will be on ways that you can improve what you've written but I won't read the same section two or three times. Otherwise we get into that grey area of whose work is being sub-mitted for final assessment, yours or mine? That's why you need someone else to read the final draft.'

'So what would they be looking for?'

'Good question. But first you need to consider how to select a critical friend. Don't ask your partner or best friend. Neither is likely to be as frank or critical as you need. It is also likely that they will have no understanding of what is required to produce a successful report. It is also one sure way to end a beautiful relation-ship.'

As Richard spoke I had visions of my ex-partner reading my assignment. It was very easy to imagine the rows that would have ensued.

'Instead see if there is someone on the course who you respect and get on with and negotiate with them a "buddy relationship" where they read your work and you read theirs. As for what your buddy should look out for, firstly make sure that they have a copy of the assessment criteria. As you know, ours are in the Course

Handbook. Secondly, identify your weaknesses. If you know, that your use of English is problematic ask your friend to pay particular attention to the clarity of expression, grammar and syntax. If you tend to be verbose ask them to highlight any padding, or if you don't trust your powers of analysis ask them to concentrate on that.'

'That sounds a bit like peer observations where you identify which elements of the lesson you want your colleague to assess,' I said.

'Exactly! But while we are on this don't forget that you can also enlist the aid of the Student Support Team (SST). We were one of the first universities to have such a team and now most colleges and universities have one. They'll read your report and comment on the structure, how logically organised the material is and your use of English. But because they are a non-specialist staff they won't comment on the content of your work.'

Richard took another sip of his coffee before continuing, 'However, you must always remember that whether you use a critical friend or the SST you are ultimately responsible for what you submit. Therefore I strongly recommend that when you complete writing, editing and checking your assignment you put it in a drawer for a week and forget all about it. Then take it out for one final edit. You'll be amazed at what you find. Along with convoluted and poorly phrased sentences, missing words, underdeveloped ideas and quotes that aren't linked to anything you will discover some really good writing. You will also find clever ideas and good examples of analysis and linking theory to practice which you can expand on further. But you will only spot these if you give yourself time to stand back from the work and review it with fresh eyes.'

Sam's reflection

22 January

I know just who I'm going to ask to be my critical friend. Let's hope that no one else has grabbed her! I should have organised this earlier. I've used buddies in the past to assess my teaching and I know how useful they can be when you get the right one. But I did have that horrible experience with Ben who seemed intent on only pointing out my failures. I can do without that. I doubt that I'll bother with the SST. Based on the comments on previous assignments my use of English and organisational skills are fine.

I do like the idea of putting the assignment in a drawer for a week before I do the final edit. But that means that I have to build this delay into my timetable. If I'm going to do it I probably need to allow about 10 days for it in total.

Review of tutorial

'One error that will significantly reduce your mark is if you report what writers have said rather than explain their ideas.'

'Sorry, I don't understand what you mean.'

'I'm not surprised. I always seem to have trouble explaining this problem clearly. Let me give you an example. A student might write: "Charles Handy (1991) in his seminal book *The Gods of Management* describes four organisational cultures. These can be compared with the eight that Morgan (1997) outlines in his book *Images of Organisations*." That statement tells me nothing about the 12 organisational cultures that Handy and Morgan describe. Nor does it allow me to assess the writer's understanding of the theories in question. The information provided could have been taken from the blurb on the back of the book.'

'So what you're saying is that I must demonstrate my familiarity and understanding of the theories and not just report their existence.'

'Precisely. What is required is something like "Handy (1991) suggests that in any organisation there are four types of cultures. These are Club, Role, Task and Individual". You would then define and explain each culture before . . .'

'Doing the same with Morgan and only then compare and contrast the two theories,' I suggested.

'Yes, so in effect you're demonstrating your understanding of the writers' theories.

Which reminds me, never discuss a theory that you don't fully understand because ...'

'Because it is better to stay quiet and have people think you are a fool than open your mouth and confirm it,' I suggested.

Richard laughed and asked, 'Who was it that said that?'

'I'm not sure but it was my mother's favourite saying.'

'While we're talking about writers it's useful to avoid starting nearly every paragraph in the Literature Review with a writer's name. For example you could rewrite the above reference to Handy as follows: "In any organisation there are four types of cultures, but what makes each organisation's culture unique is how these four are mixed. These sub-cultures are Club, Role, Task and Individual. A role culture is one in which etcetera (Handy 1991)." Can you see that by placing the reference after the explanation you're making the material your own while at the same time fully acknowledging where the ideas have come from. Try it on some of the passages in your literature review and you will be amazed at how much more authoritative your prose will sound.'

'OK I'll give it a try,' I said, not at all convinced that it would make much difference.

'The last point that I would like to raise is the need to produce an assignment that's logically structured. Although you're writing an academic report you are also telling the story of your research. A good writer will take the reader by the hand and lead them through the story, emphasising what is important, explaining complex issues in simple terms and making it as easy as possible for the reader to understand the arguments. In each chapter you must present your argument in a logical and methodical order with one point or issue leading on to the next.'

'But there are numerous logical ways to present information, for example chronologically or by theme. How do I know which is the best way?'

'Unfortunately you don't. That judgement is down to you and with experience you'll get better at it. Very often the nature of your study and the data you have influences the precise structure. What you must ensure is that if asked you can explain and justify your decision.'

'Anything else?'

'I suggest that at the start of each chapter you briefly outline its contents, then discuss the contents and end with a short summary of what the chapter was about and provide a lead into the next chapter.'

Sam's reflection

23 January

I rewrote several paragraphs from my draft literature review and put some of the references at the end of sentences. I was amazed at how much difference it made. Suddenly it seemed as if I was a full partner in the ideas discussed, rather than just repeating what the 'master or mistress' had said. I'll definitely use this approach in all my future work.

As for logically structuring my work, I should be OK on that front. Mind you, what's logical to me might not be logical to the marker. I remember a teacher at junior school asking 'when should you cross the road, when the traffic lights are on green or red?' I was the only one in the class who said red. And no matter what she or anyone else said I stuck by my answer. I was only seven but I knew I was right. It was years later before I realised what had caused the confusion. I crossed the road when the red lights stopped the traffic, rather than when pedestrians were given the green light! My logic was impeccable but not everyone understood it. So maybe I'll ask my critical friend to confirm that the work is as logically structured as I think it is.

I like the idea of writing a short introduction and conclusion for each chapter. It means that I can look at the report as five interlinked pieces of work, each complete in its own right, but also forming part of a bigger whole. Besides, although I believe in learner-centred teaching I definitely subscribe to the teaching model of 'tell 'em what you are going to teach. Tell 'em. Tell 'em what you've told them.' Even so, who'd have thought that it was also the best way to communicate academic work?

Review of tutorial

'Have a look at the handout for other issues worth addressing, but for now let's move on to your questions.'

Despite my best efforts I had failed to come up with a long list of questions and those I had didn't seem particularly important. But determined to clarify anything I didn't understand I asked, 'A problem I have is deciding what material goes in the assignment and what goes in the appendix?'

'This causes many students problems. If the information is essential to your argument then it should go in the text. But where the information is of interest but not essential it can go in the appendices. For example, if you had an organisation chart which you kept referring to in the text then I would include the table in the text. But if the chart was mentioned just once and was only intended to provide a quick overview of the organisation, I'd be tempted to relegate it to the appendices.'

'But I've read several reports where all the tables and charts are relegated to the appendices. Is that wrong?'

'I'd have to look at the specific report to answer that. But I find it very annoying when reading a report to have to keep turning over to the appendices to check on a figure or result that the writer is referring to. So . . .'

'Make it easy for the reader and put it in the text.'

'Exactly! Markers will look at appendices but I suspect that some may pay less attention to the appendices than to the main body of the report. If it is important information that you want to highlight, put it in the text.'

'Sometimes I put information in the appendices simply to stay within the word limit.'

'I've done that myself. But that shouldn't be the sole basis for your decision. If it's relevant and important it should be in the main body of the text. However, you can always summarise something in the text and provide the full details in an appendix. This is a good halfway house approach that can be of real help if you are faced with a shortage of words.'

'I don't think you can answer this question but what constitutes "enough analysis"?'

'That is a tough question and it varies depending on the level you are working at. For a first year undergraduate I would be looking for a description of the data and a minimum of one explanation of what it means. For a second or third year student I would expect alternative explanations of the data. These don't have to be diametrically opposed views of the data. They might just look at the data from slightly different angles or use different theories to illuminate the same data. For some pieces of data you may produce two or three interpretations, for others only one. In reality what we are looking for is evidence that you've thought about the data and tried to understand what it might mean in the context of your research project.'

'Does this mean that if you were doing postgraduate work you would need three or four interpretations of the data?'

'Not really. I've tried to provide a simple answer to what is a very complex question. At MA or PhD level it's not so much a question of how many alternative explanations you come up with, although they are useful, but the depth to which you have pursued your analysis. It is possible to follow one line of reasoning or analysis a very long way. But ultimately you are always limited by the number of words at your disposal. Certainly in the findings section I always worry if I don't see any citations as it's likely that reference hasn't been made to the literature review. This 'closing the loop' is absolutely vital.'

'OK so as far as analysis goes I need to avoid providing a purely descriptive report. I need to think about alternative meanings and use the Literature Review as a source of these.'

'Correct. Now the conclusion and recommendations. I use the "rule of three" for the conclusion. Firstly, try to think of the three most significant things that you've learned during your research and consider how you think practice should change as a result. Secondly, remember to identify any weaknesses in your research and how you would change your research approach if you were to repeat the exercise. Thirdly, identify areas for further study.'

'The rule of three,' I mused.

'Well, maybe for a dissertation you might go to five or so, but you get the idea. Try to be selective and concentrate the discussion on the most important things. Don't introduce any new ideas or references at this stage.'

'But how do I know if what I've written is good enough to pass?'

'In terms of the standard of your work you'll have received feedback from me. A good supervisor will discuss the quality of your work and tell you if there is a problem. They may even suggest that you seek help from the Student Support Team. But as you have no problems in terms of the general standard of your work, what you have to ensure is that you meet the assessment criteria. You should be able to check this for yourself prior to submission.'

'How?'

'Come on, you're a teacher. All you have to do is get a copy of the marking criteria which you can find in the "Course Handbook". It is then just a matter of checking that you've addressed each of the criteria in your assignment. You may find it difficult to assess the level at which you've met the criteria but it should be relatively easy to confirm that you've dealt with each criterion. For example, one of the criteria that you have to meet is linking theory to practice. A quick review of your Findings will show how often you've used the literature to explain, explore and challenge your findings.'

'Do many students check their work against the criteria?' I asked sounding defensive.

'No, unfortunately. Yet it's so simple to do. You can use the criteria like a checklist to ensure that that you've addressed all the required elements of the assignment.'

'OK,' I said. 'I'll give it a try. My last question is one that's been bugging me for a while. What do I do if the data provide totally unexpected answers? I don't for a moment think it will but ... !'

'If it does then you celebrate. Unexpected findings are the sort that researchers die for. Every researcher wants to collect data that confounds expectations. But before you get too excited you need to check that your data collection, analysis and interpretation haven't been corrupted in some way. If you're happy that they have not then you can luxuriate in the knowledge that your personal bias has had limited effect on your data gathering efforts and that what you've found is likely to be of significant interest to you, your participants, your supervisor and perhaps the wider research and professional communities of which you are a part. Now that is a wrap, so good luck!'

Sam's reflection

25 January

Well I don't expect to find that my data have confounded my expectations, so I doubt that I'll be making any claims for the discovery of new knowledge in the near future.

Appendices still bother me. It's alright saying that if the material is essential it goes in the body of the report. My question is how do you know if it is essential? Thinking about it, I suppose it all comes down to the focus of my research questions and the case that I can make in my own head, and in the report, for inclusion of the data. It's a judgement call and I'm bound to get some of them wrong. Besides, I can ask for feedback from my supervisor and critical friend, so I should be OK. Where I can't make up my mind I could consider providing a summary of the data in the text and refer the reader to the appendices for the full-fat version.

As with the use of appendices, the level of analysis required is a judgement call. Hang on I've just had a 'ping' moment. Last week I was listening to Carol in the staff room and she said that one way to measure a child's creativity was to ask them to list as many uses as possible for an everyday object, such as a brick. The more uses the more creative potential the child had. I can see some problems with that theory. But what I could do is look at my key findings and challenge myself to list a minimum of three interpretations for each and then decide which to use in my report. That reminds me of Richard's 'rule of three' for the conclusion. That's going to take some thought.

I'll miss my chats with Richard. I've learned a lot about research. But I can't wait to complete my project and get my life back.

Record of tutorial

Student: Sam Sylon　　　　　　　　　　　　　　**Date: 21/01/XX**

SUMMARY OF KEY LEARNING POINTS

- Whenever possible ask a critical friend to review your work prior to submission.

- Clearly identify which aspects of your work you want your critical friend to concentrate on.

- Review the range of services offered by the Student Support Team and decide if you wish to avail yourself of any.

- Demonstrate your understanding of any theory that you use.

- Don't use or reference a theory that you don't fully understand.

- Write assertively. Make the material you use your own. Move references from the start to the middle or end of paragraphs.

- Ensure that your work shows consistency and is structured in a logical manner with a beginning, middle and an end.

- Consider carefully what material should be included in the body of the report, included as an appendix and excluded entirely. If the information is central to your argument include it in the text.

- Look for alternative interpretations of the data. Be critical of your own thinking and theories.

- Make sure that you regularly refer to and reference sources from your literature review in your findings section.

- Remember to focus on key issues for the conclusions and recommendations. The rule of three. No new material at this stage.

- Your supervisor will tell you if your work is below the required standard. Respond positively to any advice they give you and ensure that your final assignment addresses all of the required assessment criteria.

- Welcome unexpected findings but check that they have not arisen because of a weakness in your research methodology.

Agreed action points

Sam will:

- Negotiate with a fellow student to act as each other's critical friend. Brief your friend on the areas of your assignment to which you would like them to pay particular attention.

- Obtain two copies of the assessment criteria, one for your critical friend and one for your own use.

- Check that all aspects of the assessment criteria are covered by the completed assignment prior to submission.

- Use the handout overleaf as a checklist when carrying out a final edit and polish.

The research process – putting it all together

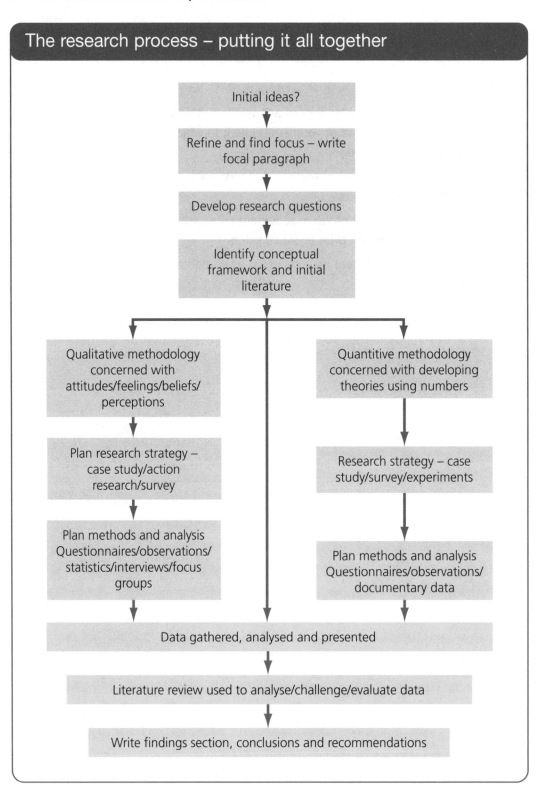

Initial ideas?

Refine and find focus – write focal paragraph

Develop research questions

Identify conceptual framework and initial literature

Qualitative methodology concerned with attitudes/feelings/beliefs/perceptions

Quantitive methodology concerned with developing theories using numbers

Plan research strategy – case study/action research/survey

Research strategy – case study/survey/experiments

Plan methods and analysis Questionnaires/observations/statistics/interviews/focus groups

Plan methods and analysis Questionnaires/observations/documentary data

Data gathered, analysed and presented

Literature review used to analyse/challenge/evaluate data

Write findings section, conclusions and recommendations

Handout

CHECKLIST FOR FINAL EDIT OF YOUR RESEARCH REPORT

Your first duty as a writer is to communicate clearly your ideas to the reader. No matter how good or original your ideas are, if your reader cannot understand what you have written they will not be convinced by your arguments. The following is a list of deceptively simple questions which you should keep in mind as you write and edit your research report. By the time you hand in your final report you should be confident that you have addressed all the questions.

- Is the content of each chapter in your report logically structured with one topic leading smoothly onto the next?
- Is the report logically structured? The reader should feel as if they are on a journey of exploration which is clearly signposted and which contains no surprises. This means that the research questions posed should determine which areas of literature are reviewed, the content of the data to be collected and method of collection. The findings should summarise, interrogate, interpret and present accurately the data in the context of the literature and the conclusions should flow naturally from them.
- Unless it is absolutely impossible, word-process your own work. The more you are engaged with your work the better. As you type you will be thinking, analysing and understanding your data. You will also be able to type and retype your work until you are satisfied. If you use a typist you are unlikely to ask them to carry out multiple retypes.
- Does the report contain a balance of description, analysis and critical evaluation or is it primarily descriptive?
- Are there any ideas or issues raised in the report that are not adequately developed? If they are important expand on the issues; if they are unimportant remove them.
- Have you used excessively long quotations in the literature review?
- Have you referenced all materials correctly?
- Have subheadings been used effectively within chapters to emphasise important issues and aid the reader's journey through the text?
- Does each paragraph only discuss one issue or idea? ➡

- Have all tables, figures and appendices been given a number, a title and a legend?
- Are there any incomplete sentences or missing words in the text?
- Does the report contain any sentences that are longer than 20 words? If so is their meaning clear?
- Has each page of the text been numbered?
- Have you used any words, phrases or theories in the report which you don't **fully understand**? If so double check that your interpretation is correct.
- Has your supervisor read and commented on your draft assignment? If yes have you implemented the changes that they recommended?
- Has your critical friend read and commented on your final draft?
- Has each page been numbered?
- Have you carried out a final edit and polish on the report?

Additional information on the issues covered by this tutorial can be found at/in:

- www.pearsoned.co.uk/colesmcgrath
- Denscombe, M. (2008) *The Good Research Guide (3rd ed.).* McGraw Hill: Maidenhead, Ch.15.
- Newby, P. (2010) *Research Methods for Education*. Longman, Pearson: Harlow, Ch. 14.

Glossary of terms

The terms used in research have never been codified. This means that they vary, to some extent, from book to book. This can be confusing. The following glossary defines how each of the listed terms has been used in this book.

Action research A cyclical process concerned with continuous improvement in which the researcher seeks to improve their professional practice by implementing a series of small interventions and monitoring the impact that each has.

Alternate hypothesis A hypothesis which states that the independent variable affects the dependent variable.

Analysis The act of breaking down a theory or data into its component parts.

Audit trail The provision of sufficient information in the final research report for the reader to understand why, how and what the researcher did.

Authentic data Naturally arising evidence.

Baseline data Data collected to inform an action research intervention.

Bias The effect of the researcher's or participants' predispositions on findings.

Boundary The limits of a particular aspect of a case study.

Case study A detailed description and analysis of an instance/phenomenon using multiple data collection methods.

Causal relationship An intervention that can be directly linked to a change in behaviour.

Chart Usually used to represent discontinuous data – a bar or column chart.

Chi squared Statistical test used to determine the probability that observed results are significantly different from expected results.

Conceptually based research Research that explores issues through the ideas and writings of others.

Conceptual framework The framework that researchers construct in their literature review from the theories of others. This is then used to explain, explore and challenge the data they collect.

Continuous data Data that can be represented on a number scale such as height.

Correlation The relationship between the independent and dependent variable. There may be no correlation, a positive or negative correlation.

Critical The process of judging the arguments presented by others and your own ideas. Unwillingness to accept at face value the views of others.

Demographics Characteristics of the population such as gender, age and ethnicity.

Dependent variable The variable that is measured.

Descriptive statistics Basic manipulation of data, e.g. percentage, mean, mode, median.

Discontinuous data Data falling into categories such as gender.

Documentary research The use of primary and secondary data contained in documents.

Empirical Research based upon the collection of data from participants or experiments.

Ethics The social, moral and professional conventions and beliefs that underpin the basis upon which research should be carried out.

Ethnography Research strategy investigating the behaviour of people(s).

Evaluation The appraisal given to a theory or interpretation of data prior to making a judgment on its value.

Figure Anything that isn't a table, e.g. chart, diagram, picture.

Focal paragraph A paragraph summarising the aims and approach to be taken in the research project.

Focus group Group of people, usually no more than 8, brought together to discuss a series of questions relating to the research focus.

Generalisable The extent to which the findings from a piece of research will be found in all similar situations.

Graph Usually used to represent continuous data – a line graph.

Grounded theory A research approach involving the development of theory following the gathering of data.

Histogram A chart showing a frequency distribution.

Hypothesis A prediction and/or supposition.

Ibid Literally 'as above'.

Independent variable The variable that is changed.

Instance Term used to describe and help define the boundaries of a case study in terms of people, organisations and events.

Intervention A change initiated as part of an action research project.

Interviews A guided discussion with the intent of obtaining relevant information from the interviewee.

Likert scale Usually a 5 point scale used in questionnaires to evaluate strength of opinion for or against a statement.

Mean Sum of the numbers divided by the number of numbers.

Median The middle number of a set.

Mode The most common number in a set.

Non-participant observation The observation of an event or process by an individual who takes no part in the proceedings.

Normal distribution Data clustered around a mean – a bell-shaped curve.

Null hypothesis A hypothesis which states that the independent variable has no effect on the dependent variable.

Paradigm A philosophical or theoretical framework. A way of thinking and organising ideas into a coherent pattern.

Participant observation The observation of an event or process by someone who is taking part in the process as part of their everyday duties.

Phenomenology An approach to studying the conscious experience of events from the perspective of the individual.

Pie chart Circular chart used to show percentages.

Plagiarism The act of passing off someone else's work as your own.

Population The entire set or group.

Primary data Raw or unprocessed data.

Probability The likelihood of something happening.

Qualitative research Research that is concerned with the attitudes, beliefs, feelings, interpretations and perceptions of participants and understanding the realities that they inhabit.

Quantitative research Research that is concerned with measurement of the phenomena under review and discovery of a single reality.

Questionnaires A set of written questions issued to a selected group.

Range Lowest number subtracted from the highest number in a set of data.

Reflective journal An evaluative record of research progress.

Relatable The degree to which findings in one location may be relevant to other similar situations.

Reliability The degree to which the same results would be obtained if the research or experiment were repeated.

Research A logical process using data and/or theory to increase the researchers understanding of the phenomena under investigation.

Research focus A statement which specifies clearly which aspects of the phenomena are to be investigated.

Research methodology A term used to describe the entire approach adopted by the researcher or just the philosophy that underpins the work, e.g. a quantitative or qualitative methodology.

Research questions A series of statements specifying precisely what the researcher hopes to discover more about.

Research strategy The structure into which the research methods used fit, e.g. action research, case studies and surveys.

Samples That part of the entire population selected to take part in the research.

Scatterplot Graph used to determine whether there's a relationship between two variables

Secondary data Processed data, e.g. percentages.

Significance A difference between two means is said to be significant if there's a less than five per cent, or point zero five, likelihood of it being due to chance alone.

Summary statistics See descriptive statistics.

Standard deviation A quantitative measure of the variability of data.

Student's t-test Statistical test used to determine the probability that two means are significantly different.

Survey The collection of data from a large number of participants, usually at a single point in time, with the intention of establishing what the current situation is.

Synthesis The process of taking the component parts of a theory or data obtained from analysis, and reassembling the parts into something new and/or different.

Triangulation The use of two or more methodologies, methods, researchers, categories of respondent, or time periods.

Validity The degree to which the research has measured/explored the phenomena that it set out to study.

Bibliography

Bell, J. (1995) *Doing Your Research Project*. Open University Press: Buckingham.

Cohen, L., Mannion, L. and Morrison, K. (2007) *Research Methods in Education* (*6th ed.*) Routledge Falmer: London.

Crotty, M. (2003) *The Foundations of Social Research: Meaning and Perspective in the Research Process*. Sage Publications: London.

Davis, P. (2007) *The Goldilocks Enigma*. Penguin: London.

Denscombe, M. (2008) *The Good Research Guide (3rd ed.)*. McGraw Hill: Maidenhhead.

Handy, C. (1991) *Gods of Management*. Century Business: London.

Hockey, J. (1993) 'Research Methods – Researching Peers and Familiar Settings'. *Research Papers in Education* Vol. 8 No. 2, pp. 199–225.

Morgan, G. (1997) *Images of Organisation (2nd ed.)*. Sage: London.

Newby, P. (2010) *Research Methods for Education*. Longman, Pearson: Harlow.

Robson, C. (1993) *Real World Research*. Blackwell: Oxford.

Wilson, E. (2009) *School-based Research: A Guide for Education Students*. Sage: London.

http://www.bera.ac.uk/guidelines. *Revised Ethical Guidelines for Educational Research*.

www.pearsoned.co.uk/colesmcgrath.

www.oecd.org.

www.scholar.google.co.uk

Index

Introductory note

This index is arranged in a word-by-word alphabetical format with set-out subheadings. It includes the tutorial discussions, reflective journal entries, summaries, diagrams, handouts and the glossary, but not the reading lists, bibliography or introductory pages. Locators refer to page numbers, and glossary entries are indicated by bold characters e.g. **191**.

abstracts in research reports 20, 28
academic writing 18–19, 29, 40, 50, 54, 158
action research 84–8, 89–90, 93, **189**
analysis, *see* findings and analysis
anonymity of participants 61, 62, 100, 135
appendices 8, 108, 180, 183
assignment criteria 175–6, 181, 182
attitudes and opinions, *see* qualitative research
audit trails 64–5, 70, **189**
authentic data 61, 62, 63, 89, **189**

bar charts 141, 155, 156, 165, 167, 169
baseline data in action research 84, 85–6, **189**
BERA (British Educational Research
        Association) 14, 61
bias **189**
    in data collection tools 83, 88–9, 120
    in findings and analysis 70
    in literature review 41, 70
    in research methodology 69–71, 72
bibliographic references, *see* references
boundaries in case studies 81–3, **189**
British Educational Research Association
        (BERA) 14, 61

case studies 81–3, 89–90, 92–3, **189**
charts 141, 155–7, 163, 167–71, **189**
Chi squared test 163–4, **189**
child protection 61
citation indexes 41
citations 40–1, 47–8 *see also* references
codes and coding systems, *see* data codes
        and coding systems

collection of data, *see* data collection
column charts 155, 163, 169–70
computer packages 43, 49, 123 *see also* Excel
        for quantitative data analysis
conceptual framework **189** *see also* literature
        review
conclusions in research reports 28, 30–1, 34, 181
consent of participants 61, 62, 109–10, 123–4
consistency in data presentation 141–2
constant comparison 137
continuous and discontinuous data 152–3, 155,
        156, 165, **189**, **190**
correlation between variables 156, **189**
critical evaluation **189**
    of data collection tools 119–20
    in literature review 23–5, 40, 45–6, 177
    of own research 31, 65, 175–6

data analysis, *see* findings and analysis
data codes and coding systems 133–4, 143
data collection, *see also* documents for data
        collection; interviews; observations;
        questionnaires
    bias in 83, 88–9, 120
    critical evaluation in 119–20
    personal contact with participants 98–100,
        112, 124
    questions link to research questions 104,
        106–7, 122
    for surveys 88–9
data gathering, *see* data collection
data protection 61, 62
data types in quantitative data analysis 152–3

databases, *see* computer packages
descriptive statistics 153, 168, **190**
diagrams 142, 148
diaries, *see* reflective diaries
discursive presentation 140
disseminating findings 8, 60
documents for data collection 118–20, 125–6

electronic sources 40–1, 54
EndNote referencing software 43, 49
ethics **190**
    guidelines 14, 61–2
    for participants in research 99–100
    in research methodology 61–3, 72
ethnography 90–1, **190**
evaluation, *see* critical evaluation
evidence
    in action research 86
    authentic **189** *see also* authentic data
    in findings and analysis 29
    for literature search 40
Excel for quantitative data analysis 153, 156,
    158, 161

figures 49–50, 157, 165, 180, **190** *see also*
    charts; diagrams; graphs; tables
final submission of research reports 176, 184–
    5, 187–8
findings and analysis 24, **189** *see also*
    qualitative research; quantitative
    research
    amount required 180–1
    bias in 70
    disseminating 8, 60
    references in 30
    research questions as headings 39
    in research reports 28–30, 33–4
    unexpected findings 182
    use of literature review 29
focal paragraphs 6, 21, **190**
focus groups 89, **190**
focus of research, *see* research focus
following up ideas, use of references in 30, 47

generalisability 57, 59–60, **190**
Google Scholar 40–1, 119

Gosset, William Sealy 161
government sources 39, 54, 119
graphs 155, 156, 158–9, 168–9, **190**
grounded theory 91, **190**

Harvard System (of referencing) 30, 48–9
highly structured data collection tools, *see*
    structured data collection tools
histograms 155, 165, 167, 170, **190**
hypotheses 154–5, 160–2, **189**, **190**

ibid 47, **190**
index cards 43, 49
insider research 8–9, 70, 75
instances in case studies 81–2, **190**
Internet, *see* electronic sources
intervention 84–7, **190**
interview questions 8, 104–7
interviewing technique 108
interviews 7–9, 102–3, 112–13, 114, 115, **190**
    characteristics shared with observations 101–2
    qualitative analysis 132–6
    questions 8, 104–7
    for surveys 88–9
    technique 108
introductions in research reports 20–1, 22–3,
    28, 32
issues, *see* themes and issues

journals 39, 40, 41, 54

leading questions 104–5
legal requirements 61
legends, use with tables and figures 50, 157
library, use for literature search 41–2
Likert scale questions **190**
    presentation of data from 58, 141, 147
    for quantitative data analysis 58, 151, 162–4
line graphs 156, 165, 167, 169
literature review, *see also* literature search
    bias in 41, 70
    critical evaluation 23–5, 40, 45–6, 177
    organising 42–5
    references 23, 47–9
    research questions as headings 39
    in research reports 23–5, 28, 32

themes and issues 43–4, 45
using quotes 23, 44
writing a 23–5, 38–54, 177–8
in writing up findings 29
literature search 38–42, 51, 53, 54

mean averages 153, 154, 158–9, 160, 163, **191**
median averages 154, **191**
mode averages 154, **191**

normal distribution 155, **191**
null hypothesis 160–2, **191**
number of interviews and interview questions 8,
    105
number of questions 105
numbers and quantities, analysis of, *see*
    quantitative research

observations 109–15
    characteristics shared with interviews 101–2
    qualitative analysis 138–9, 144
    for surveys 89
open-ended questions 5, 101, 103
organisation of literature 42–5
output from interviews 8, 105

participant and non-participant observations
    109–10, 139, **191**
participants in research
    access to 8–9
    ethics 61–3, 99–100, 135
    personal contact with 98–100, 112, 123–4
percentage make-up of research report 28
percentages, use of in presenting qualitative
    data 141–2
periodicals, *see* journals
phenomenology 91, **191**
pictures 142–3
pie charts 156, 165, 167, 171
plagiarism 30, 44, 47, **191**
planning a research project 4–15
presentation
    of data
        qualitative 140–3, 144, 146–8
        quantitative 155–9, 162–4, 165, 167, 168–71
    of research report 36, 178–9

primary and secondary data 152, 165, **191**
probability 159–62, 163, **191**
provenance of authors and sources 40

qualitative research **191**
    affected by bias 69
    data analysis 132–48
    ensuring reliability 64–5
    and generalisibiltiy 57, 60
    presentation of data 140–3, 144, 146–8
    versus quantitative research 56–9, 64, 72
    as a research methodology 72, 74
    and triangulation 67–8
quality guarantee, use of references 30, 47
quantitative research **191**
    affected by bias 69
    data analysis 150–71
    and generalisibiltiy 57, 60
    presentation of data 155–9, 162–4, 165, 167,
        168–71
    versus qualitative research 56–9, 64, 72
    as a research methodology 72, 74
    and triangulation 67
questionnaires 121–5, 126–7, **191**
    in appendices 8
    qualitative analysis 138–9, 144, 162–4
    quantitative analysis 58
    response rates 123–4
    for surveys 88
    types of question 5, 121–3, 128–9
questions, *see* interview questions;
        questionnaires; research questions
quotes, use of 23, 44, 49, 134–5, 146

range 153, 154, **191**
recommendations, in research reports 31, 181
references, *see also* citations
    in findings 30
    in literature review 23, 47–9
    purpose of 30, 44, 47
reflective diaries **191**
    in action research 84–5, 86
    in observations 111, 139
relatable research 60, 82, **191**
reliability 64–5, 70, 72, **191**
research findings, *see* findings and analysis

research focus 4–5, 11, 13, 14, **192** *see also* focal paragraphs

research methodology **192** *see also* qualitative research; quantitative research

bias in 69–71, 72

choosing a 56–9

definition in these tutorials 79

ethics 61–3, 72

generalisability 59–60, 191

in research reports 25–8, 33

triangulation 67–9

validity 63–4

research process 79, 80, 186, **191**

research questions **192**

designing the 5–7, 11–12, 13, 21, 64

link to

data collection questions 104, 106–7, 122

findings and analysis 39

literature review 39

research reports, *see also* individual sections

action research reports 86

final submission of 176, 184–5, 187–8

improving 174–88

percentage make-up 28

presentation of 36, 178–9

recommendations 31, 181

standard required 181–2

structure of 19–36, 178–9

weaknesses in 22, 31, 176

writing styles 18–19, 178–9, 187–8

research strategies **192** *see also* action research; case studies; surveys

choosing a 79–80, 95

definition in these tutorials 79–80

other strategies 90–2

research subjects, *see* participants in research

respondents, *see* participants in research

response rates for questionnaires 123–4

sampling 59–60, 65–7, 72, **192**

scatterplots 156, 168–9

searching for literature, *see* literature search

self-improvement, through action research 84, 85

semi-quantitative data 58, 162–4

semi-structured data collection tools 101–2,

103, 105, 139

significance 159–60, **192**

software packages, *see* computer packages

sources

of documents as data collection tools 118–20

for literature search 38–42, 51, 53, 54

spread of data, for quantitative data analysis 158–9

standard deviation 158–9, **192**

standard required for research report 181–2

statistical methods 153–7

statistical sources 119–20

statistical tests 160–1, 163–4

statistics 153–171

strategies, research, *see* research strategies

structured data collection tools 101–2, 103, 121

structuring a research report 19–36, 178–9

student support, accessing 176

Student's t-test 161, 162, 163, **192**

surveys 88–90, 92, 93, **192**

synthesis 23–4, **192**

tables 49–50, 140–1, 146–7, 155, 157, 180

themes and issues

in literature review 43–4, 45

in qualitative analysis 133–6, 138–9

timing

of qualitative data analysis 136–8, 143–4

of research project 10, 14

titles

in research reports 20, 21–2

use with charts 157

triangulation 67–9, 72, 82–3, 89, **192**

unexpected findings 182

unstructured data collection tools 101–2, 103, 121, 138–9

validity 63–4, 68, 72, 82–3, **192**

variables 154–6, 160, **190**

weaknesses in research report 22, 31, 176

websites 39, 40, 41, 54

writing, academic, *see* academic writing

writing styles for research reports 18–19, 178–9, 187–8